STORIES OF A SALVATION

Tim and Kimberly Jones

Contents

Preface   *v*
Introduction   *xi*

Chapter 1	Dawson Springs	1
Chapter 2	God Is On the Case	7
Chapter 3	Cigarettes	17
Chapter 4	The Insanity of the Times	27
Chapter 5	God Speaks	35
Chapter 6	Clarkston	41
Chapter 7	Phyllis and Dennis	49
Chapter 8	The Garden	55
Chapter 9	The Chief	57
Chapter 10	The Coffee House	63
Chapter 11	Two Ladies	65
Chapter 12	The Holy Ghost	67
Chapter 13	Transcendental Meditation and the Dogs	73
Chapter 14	Sunways, the Store	77
Chapter 15	The Job	83
Chapter 16	San Diego	93
Chapter 17	The Preacher with the Fire In His Eye	105
Chapter 18	The Saint Maries Fishing Trip	117
Chapter 19	The U of I	123

Conclusion   *137*
Post Conclusion   *145*

Preface

Not long ago I was in the hospital having a stress echo test for my heart. There were two technicians assisting the Doctor with preparation for the test, Julie and George. They were fun people and I found it a privilege to get to know them. It sounds odd to say that I had fun having a medical test done, but it's true, I had fun that day. George asked what precipitated my coming in for the test. I told them about how recently I was sitting in church and felt all tingly and faint and it had me worried. George asked if the experience had been an epiphany. I said no, it wasn't. I know what those are, as I have had a few in my very full life. He commented that this was his reason for avoiding church. Interesting, I thought. Does George fear an encounter with God? I wish I had asked, but the question remained locked up underneath my tongue.

With a swift redirection of the topic, George slapped some multi-syllabic words on the condition I had probably experienced that week prior. It is rare that I encounter words that I can't at least derive a semblance of meaning, but being that my expertise has always been in the engineering, electronic, technical arena, the medical terms escaped me as if they were captive birds being set free and swiftly flying off into the blue abyss. From my puzzled look George explained that the large words meant that I had experienced a near-fainting episode. He laughed as he explained that they used the large words so that I would feel better about the large bill that would be presented for the services that were provided. It was my turn to laugh, as it is all too true.

George soon was talking about heroes-- heroes from movies, heroes from real life stories. He had collected stories like trinkets from the many Veterans he had encountered in the last decade and a half of being a medical technician since his own stint as a medic in the Navy during the Gulf War encounter in Iraq. The time I had to endure the medical test evaporated like mist as I listened to George weave hero tales from the not-so-long-ago. One of George's favorite hero stories left with me that day and hovered over my head and moved down into my heart. The truth of it was profound and I began to realize how its truths resonated in even this life that saw battle on a very different battlefront and the ripple effects of those truths began to take shape in my consciousness.

The story of the American GI's taking the little seemingly insignificant island of Iwo Jima was George's favorite. Although our troops had fought against the Japanese on many islands in the Pacific before, this was the first one that was considered to be a part of the

Preface

Japanese Islands--home. The Japanese resistance was exceedingly fierce. There was much face to be saved and for them to lose this island would be very dishonorable. The General in charge of the island's defense decided to use a different tactic than the Germans used on Normandy. The Germans started firing as soon as the Allies began to land. On Iwo Jima, the Japanese held fire until the Americans were well into the landing. Then they unleashed an intense fire that trapped many in a barrage of artillery fire and machine gun fire. The advancing troops hardly knew where to step because there was no place of safety. Large numbers of men were pinned down with men dying on top of them. Then with strength and bravery mustered from deep within, some of the GI's would return fire or do something to achieve an advancement for the troops. Their actions rallied the GI's around them to also take action. The battle of Iwo Jima would eventually be won by this tactic and bold-faced bravery, with many casualties as the price.

The ones to take action in the face of intense fire, and the ones who lost life because of his action George dubbed the heroes as he concluded the story. How true! And how grateful we are to those heroes that preserved our freedom! Where would we be today without such a payment?

Those heroes on Iwo Jima remind me of my hero. Long before I was around He took action. He walked on the home turf of the enemy. He went to where the fire was most intense. He took all the artillery fire the enemy could muster, so that I would be set free from the multifaceted prison that held me captive. The enemy thought that they had defeated Him, but they were out flanked and out maneuvered by my Hero. True, the enemy did nail Him to a cross and watched Him die. But He came back. He defeated death itself that I might really live and live in freedom. He broke the bondages of addictions and of unforgiveness in me. He placed His flag of love, forgiveness, and power on my soul. He allows me to live in freedom in this life and glory in the next. Who is my Hero? Jesus. He is the Hero of heroes.

As I approached my home after contemplating what I had heard and felt on the drive home, I thought about George. Oh, George! If you only knew what I know of this hero! Your search would be complete. You would not be collecting story trinkets, but you, too would be telling stories of truth and hope! And then I recalled many other Georges I have known over the years.

Let me weave my story of redemption from the pit of hell and tell you how my Hero took me from what most would label the point of no return, picked me up, set me free, and then shared His battle strategy with me and walked into the battle with me every step of the way.

"For the eyes of the Lord range throughout the earth to strengthen those whose hearts are fully committed to him" II Chronicles 16:9

"I, the Lord, will instruct you and teach you in the way you should go; I will counsel you with my eye upon you." Psalm 32:8

"…If God be for us, who can be against us?—Who can be our foe if God is on our side? He who did not withhold or spare even His own Son but gave Him up for us all, will He not also with

Preface

Him freely and graciously give us all other things?" Rom 8:31,32 amp

Introduction

Often we liken life to a race. It seems to us a long race, but in the overall scheme of things it is but a point. Mathematically a point is defined as having no dimension, yet somehow we try to find meaning in a point on an infinite line. And in that point we will put an entire lifetime. We will be born, have our diapers changed, grow up, get a job, get married, have children, and perhaps see our children's children. Some one once said that the guy who dies with the most toys wins. But what did he win? Can he take one toy or even one dollar with him? The apostle Paul likened our life to a race with a prize in eternity.

Although this race is but a point in God's dimension of eternity, it seems from our perspective to be like a long-distance race. In the televised events of the last Olympics, I watched a long distance track race and what piqued my attention, was when the announcer said that they had started the "Bell Lap." I surmised that this was the last lap of the race. At this time most of the runners were in a pack, closely grouped together, as they had been for many laps. But now some of them started to pull away, slowly at first, as the announcer started to talk about the "kick". I surmised this "bell lap" is when the best trained committed to use ALL their reserves, and sometimes even crossed the finish line only to collapse in the arms of the one closest to them.

In our society we are not groomed to live life like the competitors run a long distance race. At some age we are expected to retire and kick back, not kick it up, pulling away to commit all our reserves to the finish of the race of life. It is almost a badge of honor to be able to retire at an early age; 60 is cool, but 58 would be better, and better yet, 55. Then what? Go fishing, play golf?

A while ago I went to Tahoma National Cemetery to pay my respects to my father-in-law. While there, I viewed many of the plaques that covered the ashes of our military personnel. One said "Gone Fishin" another said "out Golfing." My father-in-law's plaque says, "Olympic Gold". He knows something about giving it all you've got. He told stories about being in an eight-man shell, rowing with a crew known as "the great eight" and rowing until his muscles screamed in pain and his lungs burned, **and then** reaching down inside to muster more even when it seemed there was nothing left to give. To my knowledge the "great eight" still holds the record for the longest run of undefeated races in the history of rowing. He understood the concept of the bell lap.

I don't know what they will put on my plaque when I've passed on, but it sure won't be golfing or Fishing. I personally would not consider either of those to be the prize nor the race. In life, we don't hear an audible lap

Introduction

bell ring. When we should be picking up the pace, a large majority just loses motivation, get tired, or lose hope. I too, started to grow weary and decided to buy an RV, even though I knew God had told me to write a book.

Write a book? That is impossible, I thought, I don't know how to write! Just the thought of it brings back humiliating memories of my high school teacher who told me, after reading my essay that it was as though I had constipation of the brain and diarrhea of the pen. It did not matter to me that I had college degrees; I started to argue with God that I didn't know any theoretical theology and I was not capable of writing a book!

In my mind, it seemed alright that I go on an RV trip and look for items to sell on my newly developed Internet store web page. Interestingly enough, the RV burned to the ground on a remote logging road in the mountains of Idaho, 30 hours into the trip! On the drive back home, I reevaluated the direction that we were going. I have heard the bell, so to speak, so it is time I kick into high gear. Our home church is in the middle of an ambitious building program which they have entitled, "Start with the Impossible". I like that. I can relate to it. They started with the impossible, so why couldn't I? Therefore, since that day in July, my main focus has been on writing this book.

I feel that it is important that people know God works in the lives of men today, not in theoretical, but in practical ways. This is not a book of 'how to', but a book of 'He has done It!' It is a collection of stories of my salvation, and events that influenced that salvation, to the end that others might know what God is doing today, and that others not faint, but keep their faith until the end.

"But he that shall endure unto the end, the same shall be saved."
Matt 24:13 (KJV)

"If people can't see what God is doing, they stumble all over themselves;"
Prov 29:18 (MSG)

Chapter 1

Dawson Springs

Sometimes people put significance on the first memory a person can recall in their life. I can't say this is my first memory, but it is an early memory and unquestionably has had the most impact on me from my early childhood.

In the summer of 1948 when I was 5 years old I went to stay with my paternal Great Grandfather—and my namesake-- and Great grandmother Timothy Arthur and Frankie Jones in Dawson Springs, Kentucky. It was the end of World War II and my mother, a daughter of a 1st generation immigrant from Lithuania and my father, a man of Irish heritage, arrived in Dawson Springs just long enough to drop me off for the summer. I didn't know exactly why mom and dad dropped me off at Great Grandpa's house. I had never remembered seeing these relatives before in my life.

Being a War baby, I was shuffled between relatives, neighbors, and friends' houses my first few years so that my mother could work as a factory turret lathe operator in the Chicago area making parts for tanks to support us while my father served in the wartime Merchant Marines. War times were hard enough for a young boy to understand, but now was doubly perplexing. Dad had a job, mom was working in retail and the country's economy was just beginning the recovery from the war. This new predicament certainly didn't foster any feelings of importance and of being wanted.

Dawson Springs, Kentucky was a far cry from Chicago! I was dropped off at the doorstep of a small white house. The little wood house perched up on cinder blocks, high enough for little inquisitive five-year-old boys to crawl underneath, no problem. However, this particular five year old was not inclined to do this too often because I detested the bugs and spider webs that called it their domain. A small hand pump stationed next to the kitchen sink was the only form of plumbing in the house. The 'bathroom' was a 2-seater outhouse located 50 paces out back from the little house. Meals were cooked on an old coal-burning stove. Simple wood floors that were bleached parchment white from diligent scrubbing decked the house and a small porch with two cane bottom chairs graced the front door that was always open to anyone who came by. Even for 1948, the living conditions were rustic and humble. Were they a thrifty people? Downright poor would be more accurate! Poor they may have been, but dirty they were not! My Great Grandmother Frankie kept the little place tidy and spotless as if it were the Whitehouse.

My Great Grandfather, Tim Jones I., had been a

coalminer most of his working life prior to retirement. His mother had come to America from Ireland as a single mother and had worked most of her life on the King Ranch in Texas. Tim was a lean, wiry guy of tall stature. Even in retirement, he was a hard-working man, raising hogs and chickens and planting crops, well into his 70's and beyond. He had a mule named Mike. Yep, Mike the mule! He harnessed Mike the Mule to plow the field out back where he raised corn. He did his own slaughtering and hung the hog carcasses in a smoke room out back to cure. Every day or two Great Grandpa Jones walked a wheelbarrow up the hill a mile or so to the coal mine, filled it up with coal, and wheeled it home to use in the cook stove.

Great Grandpa Jones was a good man, not harsh or abrasive, but stern. He didn't take any guff from a 5-year-old upstart, I can tell you firsthand. One time he chased me up a tree after discovering I had done something mischievous. I sat on a tree limb relishing my triumph at outwitting him and escaping the punishment. But Great Grandpa, I'm afraid, got the last laugh as he stood, switch in hand, just underneath the tree and painted the more realistic picture for me: "You might as well come down, boy. I can wait a lot longer'n you can".

One day a bunch of people came over to the little white house. Great Grandpa put ice and salt into a wooden bucket, as I looked on, enthralled. Then he put another container with a handle into the first. All the kids took turns cranking the handle. After every child had a turn, Great Grandpa took the top off and everyone had a share of the most delicious ice cream I have ever tasted!

Great Grandma Frankie Jones was a hard worker as well. She awoke before the first glimmer of dawn each morning and baked biscuits for her husband's breakfast. In addition to being industrious, she was also a woman of faith. Every Sunday she walked up a dusty dirt road to a little white steeple-topped church to worship. While I was staying with them, she took me along as well. One typical hot Kentucky summer Sunday I watched my great grandmother fanning herself through the church service with her hand-held paper fan on a stick, and I remember asking myself, "What are we doing here?"

That was the beginning of the thread of God's working in my life. That simple question and the image of Great Grandma Frankie sitting there in the sweltering heat became the first of many such spiritual mile post markers in my life before I came to know God, the Father as my savior. Who knows what strikes each person as significant? For each of us it is different, but for me seeing my great grandmother sitting there in the stifling heat told me what she was doing was important enough to her to endure the heat for some reason and I wanted to understand that reason.

Over the decades, I have come to also realize that it was the prayers of this faithful relative that stood out as beacons for my soul. I am forever indebted to Great Grandma Frankie and others who laid the groundwork for my entering the Kingdom of Light, even when what they saw in the natural was anything but encouraging as I walked through some black decades and should have been dead many times over.

"The effectual and fervent prayer of a righteous man [woman] avails much" James 5:16 NKJV

Chapter 2
GOD IS ON THE CASE

When I was in the 3rd and 4th grades, I lived with my mother and her second husband, Bill Graf and was required by them to go to the local Catholic Church on Sundays. Although I saw no evidence of faith during the time I knew him, Bill had been an alter boy in the Catholic Church as a youth. He even gave me his rosary which had an intricately designed black and silver crucifix attached to it. It was a really nice piece. But I think the real reason I had to go to Catholic Church was so that Bill and my mother could sleep late on Sunday mornings without an eight year old bothering them in their tiny apartment.

I went to Catholic Church as long as it was required, no more. The lessons learned from my stepfather, were of a very different tenor. I learned that I was a bother to have around. I learned that I needed to look out for myself, because no one else would, including my mother. I learned not to show fear, but to mask it with anger so I that had a showing of strength even if I was hurting inside.

Stories of a Salvation

When I was eight years old my mother and stepfather often went out and left me in the apartment with instructions to go to sleep. I had been instructed one night to do just that and likewise I had been instructed not to mess with Bill's alarm clock radio; but with many hours alone and nothing to do, this inquisitive and headstrong boy succumbed to the temptation of turning on Bill's radio and switching it to a station that suited me. When Bill returned to the apartment in the wee hours of the morning and discovered I had messed with the radio, he was enraged! He awakened me, took me, still in my pajamas and drove me to a corner in a new housing development somewhere in Lakewood, all the while telling me how worthless I was and that I needed to be taught a lesson. At the corner in the development, he ordered me out of the car and drove off. There I was, eight years old, alone in the middle of the night and right then and there I made a resolve to never be hurt again; I would be tough and I would be in control. Although I was in a strange town, I had developed a plan in my head! I would walk to Hollywood and more specifically, to the Hollywood Roosevelt Hotel where I knew my Dad stayed when he was in town. I figured that even if Dad were not in town the hotel staff would know how to contact him. I had previously studied a road map of the LA area and knew from where I was standing I needed to go west and then north. Somehow I calculated the journey to take me a couple of days on foot, so I commenced walking. It crossed my mind that being seen in my pajamas might be awkward, but onward I resolutely trudged. A little later that night I was picked up by a very shaken Bill, who had been driving around looking for me, probably scared to death that he would catch flak from the law or my mother if he didn't return me to the apartment intact. When he asked me where I was walking to, I replied that I was just walking to stay warm, as Bill never liked it when my father was mentioned.

Another time he hit me so hard I hit my head against a wall and had to be taken to the hospital to be treated for a head laceration. I have no idea what I had done to provoke Bill in this event, but as is so often the case, a child disciplined in anger only hears the anger, not the correction. Child abuse was not widely talked about in the '50's, but I suspect my stepfather was concerned about allegations even then because he was worried I might tell the hospital staff the true events. He told me to tell them I slipped and fell.

When I was ten years old, I went to live with my father and stepmother. My father was not much better. He also was verbally and physically abusive, especially when he was drunk, which were most nights. Some of his "discipline" also landed me in the hospital with damage to my kidneys. But the far greater damage to me was what happened to my spirit.

By the time I was in Junior High School, I was tough and people did not mess with me. I didn't like to get into fights, but if I was drawn into one, believe me, I was going to make sure I won! I gained some respect from fellow students from my hot temper, maybe not the kind of respect one desires, but it was working for me. My long-time friend, Jeannie tells about how when I was in high school I passed out on the front lawn from inebriation at a party at her house and they elected to let me stay there and sleep it off all night rather than waking me and possibly encountering my wrath.

I once pulled a knife on my stepmother to threaten her over some issue whose memory has long since been lost in oblivion. This resulted in my father going to a professional for counseling. The counselor told him the problem was that he needed to spend more time with me, so my dad checked the two of us into a nice hotel for a 3-day weekend. I swam in the hotel pool and I had his attention all to myself and had a great time. I soaked it up like a human sponge. Although my dad had many faults, I desired his approval more than anything and the violent behavior toward my stepmother became positively reinforced. Dad went back to his normal routine that next week, but those few days were better than any other in my life!

Spiritually speaking by this point, I was decidedly anti-God. I saw no evidence that He existed at all in my life, however had you asked me in High School if I was an atheist, I would have replied, no. I called myself an agnostic because I saw no evidence that God existed but I also thought that it was an untenable position to argue that God didn't exist. I removed the crucifix from the rosary that Bill had given me years before and hung it upside down from a chain around my neck. Usually when I was around my mother, I wore the chain inside my shirt, but otherwise it was out where other people could see it. Some people may have thought I was advocating witchcraft, but I didn't care what others thought. Because the crucifix was out there where people could see, I was a target for anyone with the guts to make a comment, or a wisecrack. One day a guy approached me and asked if I wore the crucifix upside down to symbolize my desire to be like Peter, and be crucified upside down. He didn't stay around for an answer, almost as if he was afraid of what my reaction might be. This idea blew me out of the water! I was so shocked I was speechless and stood as if frozen to the ground for what seemed an interminably long time. This question made such an impact on me, I didn't wear the crucifix upside down anymore. Was this a smart Aleck or the Spirit of God speaking through this stranger? It provoked me to thought, needless to say.

I had a neighbor named Vicki that I hung out with in my high school years and she went to church. Sometimes she asked me to go with her and I went a number of times to check it out. One evening, the pastor gave an alter call for all to come forward for salvation. The entire youth group went forward, except for two others and me. The three of us stood like solitary rocks in a sea of empty chairs. I saw nothing to compel me to go forward that night, but I do remember having thoughts very contradictory to my declared anti-God position. I remember looking at a leaf and thinking, "there must be a God; look at His leaf". Hmm...a very peculiar and out of character thought for me to have. Another girl from that same youth group asked me to a Sadie Hawkins day dinner (equivalent to what they call Tolo now). This girl was very well built, but she did not come across as a sexy hottie, but instead had purity about her, which I was unaccustomed to seeing. After the dinner, as we were walking down the hall to go home, I reached over and took her hand, which was what I thought was the normal course of things. She shook off my touch abruptly, as though I were a leper. Having not ever encountered such a response before, I immediately presumed my hand was sweaty or something. Whatever the reason she shook off my touch, I took offense and never went back to that youth group.

During my junior year of High School, I hung out and identified with a group of seniors who called themselves the "Intellectuals". Like any High School, we had the usual social strata like the "Jocks", "Hoods", "and Socials".... but we also had distinct strata for the "Intellectuals", and those we referred to as the "Pseudo-intellectuals". Ironically, it was the group we looked down on with disdain, the "Pseudo-intellectuals" that achieved the exceptional grades. We differentiated ourselves from them by calling our group the "Intellectuals" which was comprised of some of the smartest guys that I have ever met, some of them testing at the genius level on IQ tests, the "dumbest" of the group having an IQ of 135. Several went on after High School to acquire Doctoral Degrees. My friend Steve became the Senior Statistician at the Linus Pauling Institute and then later was a Senior Program Analyst for IBM. One of the members of our little group was conducting experiments to develop a cure for cancer by introducing minuscule amounts of poison into cancerous tissue in order to kill the cancer cells, something we all now know as Chemotherapy. His senior year, he was investigated by the FBI because he tried to buy Botulinum Toxin for his research. (This was during the Cold War). We just couldn't be bothered with the busy-work necessary to get high grades; there were many more important and real issues to be concerned with!

This group of guys followed Formula One racing and we found creative, but not necessarily legal, ways to get into the Riverside Raceway without monetary consideration. We favored the European cars and the European racing circuit over the Indianapolis Racing League because Formula One racecourses were primarily road courses instead of ovals. NASCAR was not really a big item yet in our world. Road course driving took more skill, finesse, and agility of mind than ovals. Additionally, Indianapolis Racing cars were perceived to be technologically inferior by those in our group with the strongest ties to the racing world. We esteemed the Formula One drivers' agility and appreciated the intelligence, wit and gall it took to do this kind of driving as well as the intelligence it took to design these amazing cars to go fast, perform well, and push the envelope of technology. Two of my friends from this era of my life went on to become legends in their own right in the racing circuit.

When we weren't at the raceway, our group often congregated at Dan's house, since his parents were conveniently rarely home. The pastime of choice there was a 'stimulating' game of chess or conversational discourse on any of many controversial or thought-provoking topics. We prided ourselves on intellectually deep discussions and we esteemed intellect and reasoning above all else. We sat around and conversed for hours while drinking Dan's parents' expensive Vodka and Whiskey, often with Opera playing in the background. After we imbibed our fill of the expensive alcohol, we refilled the bottles with the cheap stuff we could afford and returned them to the cupboard.

    For a period of time God became the focus of the discussions. Some of my compatriots were atheists; most were agnostics, as was I. I don't recall who advocated on behalf of God, but the argument never leaned in his favor. I decided it would be best for the sake of discussion to get reinforcements for God's side, so I invited a friend that lived across the street from me who attended Catholic Seminary in lieu of public high school. My friend and Seminarian, Bill, introduced the group to the five proofs that Saint Thomas Aquinas presented in his Summa Theologiae as proofs of the existence of God. Each of the premises started with one or more assumptions. Each premise was intently listened to and then analyzed thoroughly by the group. After going around and around with each premise and all the facets were exhausted to the best of our ability, we concluded through consensus that the arguments were circular. Finally, out of exasperation, Bill advocated we all meet with a priest from the local parish, so he set up an appointment for all of us to go. Bill tried to get the priest to prove the existence of God, and the priest did try.... briefly. At first the priest looked extremely frustrated, but then his countenance relaxed and he surmised for us all that really it came down to just having **faith**. I don't know what the Intellectuals were thinking at that moment, but I knew I did not have faith and that was that! For me this settled the issue completely and I didn't have to look any more. Settled! Or so I thought.

Abuse followed me into adulthood. I became an abusive, angry man and it was many decades before I was completely delivered from that nature. But God never gave up on me. Our society today shuns those labeled as abusers. We hear terms associated with these people (usually men) such as deadbeat, hopeless, outcasts. Society, even most pastors and their churches, give up these people as beyond help, but God does not give up. He sees these people who are full of anger, pain, self-condemnation, social condemnation as beloved just like all the rest. He loved me even when I was unlovable.

The amazing thing is that although I considered the subject settled in my intellect, my heart was not satisfied and was still seeking.... something, who knows what! It was as though I began the seeking process there in those discussions with my colleagues, there in the sea of empty chairs, there in the upside down crucifix, there in the pew in Dawson Springs. I was a tough case. I had already developed a heart that was calloused and a spirit that was bashed and bruised from the abuse that I had endured from my parents and stepparents, but that didn't matter to God. He is much bigger than that.

I started something in motion just by seeking and

searching and then God was on the case to reveal Himself to me over time, and through circumstances, experiences, and people. It took Him awhile; I was a hard nut to crack, but He didn't give up, from this time on, He was on the case!

"But if from there you seek the Lord your God, you will find him if you look for him with all your heart and with all your soul." Deuteronomy 4:29

"You will seek me and find me when you seek me with all your heart." Jeremiah 29:13

"So I say to you: Ask and it will be given to you; seek and you will find; knock and the door will be opened to you." Luke 11:9

"While we were yet in weakness [powerless to help ourselves], at the fitting time Christ died for (in behalf of) the ungodly. Now it is an extraordinary thing for one to give his life even for an upright man, though perhaps for a noble and lovable and generous benefactor someone might even dare to die. But God shows and clearly proves His [own] love for us by the fact that while we were still sinners, Christ (the Messiah, the Anointed One) died for us." Romans 5:6,7, Amplified

Chapter 3

Cigarettes

I agree wholeheartedly with the infamous Mark Twain when he said," Quitting smoking is easy. I know. I've done it hundreds of times." Cigarette smoking may be on the decline in the USA, but I suspect that there are millions of addicted smokers out there that have puffed it, patched it, and white knuckled it--whether they have managed to kick the habit or not-- that would chime a resounding "Amen, brother!" to that statement. How many of my friends over the decades lamented of the struggle? I could not count.

Nowadays, with the concern of 'second hand smoke' health risks, smoking has become a social leprosy in our society. Smokers may smoke in certain areas only and must be so many feet from the entrance to buildings. What a different picture from the 1950's and 60's! The suave, debonair men and the glamorous, luscious starlets were plastered all over the movie screens in full color Cinemascope with an ice-bobbled drink in one hand and a long, slender cigarette in the other. Smoking was cool, sophisticated. Cocktail parties in smoked-filled rooms were hip. The infamous Marlborough Man, ruggedly handsome beyond belief was depicted riding a horse up some rugged terrain, pausing only to capture the landscape and puff on his cigarette. The image shouts: "How can you be a real man unless you smoke?" My, times have changed!

I smoked my first cigarette when I went to Roosevelt Elementary School, in Long Beach, California, where I attended the third and fourth grades. During recess one day, some classmates of mine asked if I wanted to go smoke a "cig". I said sure. We crept around the side of the school building and crouched down between the building and the bushes on the street side where we savored the tantalizing taboo tobacco for the first time. Those first clandestine puffs as we passed the solitary slender token from one wide-eyed boyish face to another, were exhilarating! We had just been ushered into cool-dom!

After that it became standard protocol for my buddies and I to peruse the street gutters for 'partials', cigarettes that had been discarded by adults that still had a few good draws in them. Even back then, no clerk could be persuaded to sell a package of cigarettes to a fourth grader, no matter what charm or deception was attempted so once in a while one of us mustered courage to buy a pack from a vending machine when we thought no one was looking. Our perception was that any adult would stop us from the purchase if they could, so it meant walking to the vending machine without drawing attention to oneself, inserting the quarter into the machine, pulling the selection knob, grabbing the cigarette pack, hightailing it out of there and running like hell just in case someone might be following! Of course, there was no way we were going to risk the possibility of getting caught, because then our parents knew and it was all over.

    I used to steal cigarettes from the purse of my step dad's Office Assistant when given the chance. It didn't take her long to realize that she was "smoking" more and enjoying it less. My stepfather, Bill, busted me and he was livid! He grabbed me and started dragging me, meanwhile telling me what a worthless no-good kid I was and how he was going to get rid of me. I locked my arms around the leg of a worktable that was bolted to the wall and held on for dear life. I had been the recipient of the results of his anger before and didn't dare let go! He yelled and carried on until everyone in the building came over to see what was happening and then he finally calmed down. It wasn't long after this that I was asked to go before a judge for a hearing. I don't know if my mother and stepfather had decided they had enough of me or if my mother was trying to protect me from Bill, but the end result after talking to the judge in his chambers was that I went to live with my father, new stepmother, and baby sister in Westchester, California.

    That was the end of my smoking career for quite awhile. I shared a smoke with a fellow camper when I went on a YMCA trip to the Sierras during my Junior High years. Although I was no newbie to cigarettes, the four-year abstention had done its trick and that one cigarette made me surprisingly light headed and queasy. I emphatically decided then and there I was never going to smoke!!! ...And I didn't. ...At least not for a few years!

The summer before my senior year of high school, I started working for my stepfather driving a delivery route for his photo-processing lab to process the new technology of the day, Kodacolor prints. I was one of three delivery guys employed by my stepfather and my route was Long Beach along the Pike, Torrance and then back to the plant in North Long Beach. When I reflect back, peer pressure from the guys that worked at the lab might have been a factor in my picking the habit back up. They all smoked, drank, partied heavily, and were pretty wild by late fifties' standards, especially for those under twenty-one. I went to a party once with them and was offered alcohol along with pills," yellows and reds" as they called them. Yellows and reds were barbiturates, downers. That one party was enough for me and I decided that was not my scene, but the smoking habit stuck. My reintroduction to cigarettes and a status quo with the guys bloomed into a lusty habit of almost 2 packs a day.

When I started the delivery job, it was 1959 and I was using one of my dad's cars to do the route initially, but after a few weeks of borrowing his car, he decided to buy me a Mustang. But wait, you say the Mustang didn't come out until late 1964. True, THE Mustang came out then. Almost anyone who knows Automobile History knows the Ford Mustang's historic debut on the American market. My Mustang was a British-built cross between a motor scooter and a motorcycle. It had a large single cylinder flat head engine, which for the size, was oh, so slow! Worse, it couldn't stop very fast--I don't know if it was a bad design or a bad mechanic. Worse yet, it broke a lot. One time when it broke down, Bill Graf had to run my route. It took him five hours to run a route that I did in three and after that he never complained about how long it was taking me; in fact, it was probably the best thing that could have happened for me because as a result of that delivery, he decided to buy me a car. The agreement we had was that I maintain it and pay for the gas, but he owned it. So at 18 years old, I had a company car, a '53 Plymouth with six cylinders, three speeds and overdrive. It was a dog, but it didn't howl at the moon, and it ran!

The most significant feature of that company car was that NOW, I had a place to stash my cigarettes! I still wasn't eighteen yet, but I was 6'4" and no store clerk dared card me for smokes, but I needed a place to stash them. The family never mentioned, or maybe they never knew that I smoked. My stepmother didn't smoke, but my father did, so the house already smelled of tar and nicotine, so who knows if they detected I was smoking also, but it was for darn certain that I did not want to find out and risk the effects of my dad's wrath again. I smoked before school and chain-smoked after school. A smoker doesn't like to be too far from the object of his addiction so I often carried cigarettes on to the school grounds, in spite of the risk of being caught and reprimanded.

One day, while in high school, when I went to the

liquor store to buy a pack of smokes, I found the price for a pack had risen a penny: to 22 cents a pack. I was outraged! I swore that when they hit 25 cents, I would quit. Right! I was never able to quit for such a reason as price. I suspect price has not ever been a very successful motivator for kicking the habit for most people because smokers are still smoking today with prices for a pack of cigarettes being more than ten times what I was paying back then!

After graduating from Rancho High School I enrolled at Long Beach State (notice I didn't say 'attended') where I attained a whopping .9 GPA before they kicked me out. I was working part-time at a grocery store and partying and drinking—mostly partying and drinking—and of course my smoking addiction was my constant party companion. I had a fake ID even before I turned 18, so getting alcohol was like child's play.

Eventually I moved on and obtained a job at Autonetics as a System Tester. I determined to give college another try, so I enrolled at Fullerton Junior College and subsequently Orange Coast College where I eked my GPA up to a 2.0. I was basically a ship without a direction, catching whatever windy gust of an idea came my way. I was undeclared in my major, as I didn't really have an idea of what I wanted to do and I never developed good study habits to combat my lack of discipline and chaotic lifestyle. While I was taking courses such as Calculus and German, I was working six to seven days a week (full-time plus overtime) at Autonetics and smoking upwards of three packs a day.

Cigarettes

Toward the end of this time drugs were infiltrating my life more and more, as I discovered a little amphetamine pick-me-up boosted my endurance to handle the hefty work/school/partying load. I had a girlfriend that was studying to be a pharmacist, so frequently I called her up at the pharmacy where she was interning to "get a little help from my friend". On the phone, she pretended to be talking to a doctor and took a prescription for Dexedrine 12 hour time-release capsules or sometimes tranquilizers (to take the edge off), which the pharmacy then dispensed to me. After that relationship broke up, the drug thing got worse. I began sniffing crystal methadrine and man did I smoke then! Calling it chain-smoking would be the Master of Understatement! It was like putting chain-smoking on fast-forward.

As I drifted into the drug culture, I moved more toward the hippie movement and the counterculture and farther away from mainstream working class life. I left behind the job and paycheck for a 'more free' way of life in distribution of "uppers". Money became scarce—so scarce I often didn't have money for food—but amazingly, I always had tobacco to smoke because we bought tobacco before we bought food. It seemed that it was impossible to quit. Any addiction can grow to be a voracious tyrant, exacting complete abject servitude from the enslaved, and my smoking habit was no different. There were times that we ate fried potatoes for a meal—without even onions or garlic in them! In my estimation, that is poor, because I **love** onions and garlic! (I once heard someone say garlic is like sex: you can never get too much of it. I agree wholeheartedly with that statement!) Sometimes we ate on the beach, being fed by the Diggers of Laguna Beach, an offshoot of the Diggers of Haight-Ashbury District of San Francisco who handed out free food and freely handed out their philosophy of anarchist guerrilla street theater and free association.

When my first wife was pregnant with my first child, Jennifer, I had a new surge of resolve to quit and was able to do so for quite a while. I agonized my way through nicotine withdrawal and stayed off cigarettes for about eight months before the stress of life drove me back. I had many circumstances in my favor then, as I was highly motivated to set a good example for my new baby and no one where I worked, US Polymeric, smoked. I knew that a child smoking was highly correlated to their parents' smoking and I didn't want my kids replicating that insatiable habit of mine. Heaven knows I had followed in the footsteps of my father in his smoking habit. By the time my oldest children were in their early teens, my dad's habit of smoking had taken its toll on his health and he contracted lung cancer, for which the doctors had to remove half of a lung, followed by treatment with radiation and chemotherapy. Unfortunately the small cell cancer was very aggressive and had gone to his bones, thereby releasing the calcium from his bones into the blood and he subsequently died of calcium poisoning.

Although I had no crystal ball or premonition that hinted this was going to eventually happen to my dad, I didn't like the black stuff I was coughing up in the mornings. It didn't take a premonition to tell me this was not healthy for me. Soon, I was smoking two to three packs a day again.

Shortly after Jennifer was born, we moved to Clarkston, Washington, which was right on the Washington-Idaho border. At that time we were living on Second Ave in a little rental house and were living the 'peace, love, and granola tea' lifestyle of the hippie movement. I wasn't working during these days, and money was scarce so I rolled my own cigarettes to save pennies. I accepted Jesus as Lord of my life during those first three years there. The pastor at the church I started attending talked about how we could be delivered from things that bound us up. Each morning I coughed up about a tablespoon of black tarry stuff from smoking. I knew I was bound like a chain to this addiction and I really needed to be set free from this nicotine drug once and for all!

I decided to thank Jesus for the tobacco every time I wanted to smoke. When I told my new found friends who were Christians, what I was doing they looked puzzled and perplexed. Some said, "Why do you want to thank God for something that the devil has used to bind you up?" I answered that the lack of ability to acquire the tobacco doesn't set a person free and the Bible says: " whom Jesus sets free is free indeed". The truth is that the Lord created the tobacco plant. I was the one who had misused it. So I made it a regular practice that before I smoked or rolled a cigarette, I sat down and spent some time thanking and praising God for providing me with the item to satisfy the craving for nicotine. In my heart

I knew that if He got tired of hearing me praise Him for the smokes, then, He-- not me-- would set me free from the tobacco. It wasn't long before He nudged me to put aside the tobacco; one day as I was sitting in my chair with a can of Prince Albert on the table next to me I just pushed it aside and never picked it up again. I had no craving for a smoke from that minute on, even to this day, no withdrawal, no patch, no white-knuckling it, no cold turkey. I found that Jesus is more than capable and very willing to break the generational mistakes that entangle us. He met me in my addictive need and set me free. In the past, I gave thanks for the tobacco; today I give thanks for being tobacco-free for over thirty-five years!

"In every thing give thanks: for this is the will of God in Christ Jesus concerning you." I Thessalonians 5:18 KJV

"To the Jews who had believed him, Jesus said, "If you hold to my teaching, you are really my disciples. Then you will know the truth, and the truth will set you free......So if the Son sets you free, you will be free indeed." John 8: 31,32,36 New International Version

Chapter 4

THE INSANITY OF THE TIMES

During the time I was part of the drug culture, I was using 'uppers' heavily and I developed a standard for myself that whatever the recommended amount was to get high, I took double. I used crystal meth--methadrine, speed, all the same thing-- and I used it extensively for awhile and although it is addictive, I handled the addiction very easily: I just switched to LSD! My friends and I referred to those who didn't do drugs (most of the people in society) as "lame". Oh, they might drink alcohol, but they were still lame, in fact, alcohol use or not, the "regular people" were lame. We perceived with disdain that the American Dream was "having 25% more than I have now." We viewed the establishment as being in search of the bigger car, or house, or education, but their lives were essentially dysfunctional. We used the term only for those that didn't smoke pot or take any of the myriad psychedelics available, however one day as my friend Al and I sat around smoking pot it occurred to me that the label of "lame" fit the people in the world in which we lived as well. We were a product of that society and therefore we too were lame. Those people that we labeled "lame" claimed we used drugs as a crutch. I essentially agreed with them, but at least I recognized the fact that I too, had been lame and had difficulty with functioning--indeed it was almost impossible for me to function at all with the level of alcohol that I habitually had been consuming.

    The truth is that we were all dysfunctional in our society--in fact, in the world-- each in our own way. Some felt unloved, some were perceived as frigid, some lacked creativity. For all the advancements in society through the centuries, as far as we were concerned, it had failed miserably and it was out of that despair, dissatisfaction, and disillusionment with the 'establishment' that the counterculture was birthed. Look at the number of communes that sprang up in the late sixties. People were willing to try radical lifestyles to fill that need for significant meaning in their lives and to fill the unending loneliness that persists even in a crowd. Some may know this era as the hippie, or love, peace, and granola (what I now call 'lust, what-piece-can-I-get, and granola-tea) era, but for many of us it was an all-out cultural revolution— our attempt to make right what we perceived had gone so wrong in the world. The song "Eleanor Rigby" by the Beatles so appropriately captures the essence of the loneliness and malaise of our culture during this counterculture era:

    Ah, look at all the lonely people!
    Ah, look at all the lonely people!

The Insanity of the Times

Eleanor Rigby picks up the rice in the church where a wedding has been
Lives in a dream
Waits at the window, wearing the face that she keeps in a jar by the door
Who is it for?
All the lonely people
Where do they all come from?
All the lonely people
Where do they all belong?
Father McKenzie writing the words of a sermon that no one will hear
No one comes near.
Look at him working. Darning his socks in the night when there's nobody there
What does he care ?

All the lonely people
Where do they all come from?
All the lonely people
Where do they all belong?

Eleanor Rigby died in the church and was buried along with her name
Nobody came
Father McKenzie wiping the dirt from his hands as he walks from the grave
No one was saved.

All the lonely people
Where do they all come from?

All the lonely people
Where do they all belong ?

  I went down to the San Jose Pop Festival in the late 60's. This was a time in my life when I was homeless and jobless (by choice), so it was easy to go to a happening like that. I camped outside the night before and made a few overnight acquaintances; getting there was easy, getting inside was another matter. The next day we milled around outside the entrance gate wondering how to get in with no money when one of my new acquaintances boasted, "I'm going to make myself invisible and walk right through the gate, past the ticket-takers and the guards. Did he make himself invisible? Not to me. I watched him as he walked to the gate and I watched him walk right through the gate, past the ticket takers, and the guards. Was he invisible to them? Well, not a one of them ever even gave him a glance. Today we like to explain things from a scientific point of view, but was it a miracle? Or Magic? Or just dumb luck? "Who do you serve? You've got to serve somebody. It may be the devil, or it may be the Lord. But you've got to serve somebody." As sung in "Slow Train" by Bob Dylan.
  I was still on the outside of the gate, but soon someone came and told us that there was a hole in the fence and he pointed to a craft booth next to the hole where a constant stream of people were exiting the booth, but no one was going in. So, we went to the hole and crawled through while the booth operator helped many more interlopers and us as quickly as possible.

Once we were inside the music started; I don't remember who played except the Doors with Jim Morrison being so drunk or on downers (barbiturates, heroin, or depressants) to the point of hardly being able to stand. Someone came up to me that I didn't know, and asked if I got my 'hog' yet. I said, "Man I don't own any bike, much less a Harley." He said, "Put out your hand." I did. He said," Not a Harley, these." Then he put about fifteen or twenty orange #5 capsules in my hand and disappeared into the sea of people. As soon as he left, and before I could even wonder about what these caps contained, some hippie-looking dude took the microphone on stage, and told the tens of thousands of people about a party the night before at the Carousel Ballroom in San Francisco. He described how the party was attended by Big Brother and the Holding Company with Janis Joplin (my favorite group at that time), as well as the Hell's Angles and that they had named a new drug after the Hog of the HA's. It was a new synthetic, macrobiotic, psychedelic drug and was being given away free at the festival. As I pondered how they could have a drug that was both synthetic and macrobiotic at the same time, the dude went on to announce that there were people in the crowd that had some hog and they were giving it away. "Would the people that have some hog put your hand up?" My hand shot up, without thinking about a thing. Soon I had dispensed all but two caps. I took those myself, as I always believed that I required at least a double dose.

  Fortunately I sat down on the grass before proceeding to 'turn into clay, and sink into the earth'. It might have been scary for someone that had something to live for, but I had nothing to live for. To my doper friends and me when asked why we did something our response was often, "It's something to do". Later that same day an angry guy came up to me and accused me of giving a 'hog' to his girlfriend that sent her to the emergency room. "What did you think you were doing!" he lashed at me. I looked him in the eye and told him it was an unknown substance to me and that I had taken two myself. He just said "oh," and walked away, but the 'hog' sent dozens of people to the emergency room that day. The whole day had a surreal quality about it. It was an indicator of the insanity of the times.

Previously I described how I had taken the crucifix from the ornate rosary that Bill Graf had given me, removed it from the beads, hung it upside down from a chain and wore it around my neck--not because of witchcraft, not because I was an atheist, but just because. And after leaving the Catholic Priest's office with the Intellectuals in Garden Grove California, my spiritual curiosity dried up like a prairie well as I had seen and experienced very little evidence of the possibility of a loving and caring God. I had become totally negative and anti most everything. Today when we look back at that time in my life, an old friend recaps it by saying that I was a nihilist.

***"Nihilism** (from the* Latin *nihil, nothing) is a* philosophical *position which argues that the world, especially past and current human existence, is without objective meaning,* purpose, *comprehensible* truth, *or essential* value. *Nihilists generally assert some or all of the following: there is no reasonable proof of the existence of a higher ruler or creator, a "true morality" does not exist, and* secular ethics *are impossible; therefore, life has no truth, and no action can be preferable to any other. The term nihilism is sometimes used synonymously with* anomie *to denote a general mood of despair at the pointlessness of existence."* [1] From Wikipedia

I never called myself a nihilist, but sometimes the shoe fits and we don't recognize it. At one point, I remember suggesting a course of action and someone asking why we should do it. My response was, "It's something to do." Generally, there was no 'reason' to do anything as far as I was concerned. Although I thought it futile to defend the position of an atheist, most all of my thoughts and actions would lead one to believe that I had no belief in God or a morality of any kind.

I look back on this insane time and see it as a directionless, despairing existence. We were bumbling through a lifeless life, as best we could.

"If people can't see what God is doing, they stumble all over themselves; but when they attend to what he reveals, they are most blessed." Proverbs 29:18 (MSG)

Jesus says, "I am the gate; whoever enters through me will be saved...I have come that they may have life, and have it to the full....I am the way and the truth and the life. No one comes to the Father except through me." John 10: 9,10, 14:6

Chapter 5

God Speaks

Whatever the problem, drugs were exalted as the answer. Some of the books that circulated among my friends sited specific stories where LSD could be used to heal all the problems already mentioned and many more. We recognized we had problems, and psychedelics were touted as the answer. We were going to fix our dysfunctional lives by opening our minds and getting "turned on, tuned in, and dropping out". (a phrase coined by Timothy Leary). We read about a furniture designer that had a mental block and could not create new furniture designs, however after taking a dose of acid, he came up with stupendous designs. We were led to believe diseases and maladies of all kinds could be healed through the use of psychedelic drugs, specifically LSD. Today, I realize that these remedies are counterfeits of what the Holy Spirit can do. Psychedelic drugs can bring some short-term results sometimes, but then with it also comes a deterioration of the inner man and the primordial malaise is still there. I can see this now, but at the time, I had no knowledge, much less belief in anything spiritual.

So for many others, and me, acid became the bright and shining hope of the future. With LSD I had many episodes, or experiences while high, and episodes of many different natures, but there was only one episode that had any real significance and it had a long term impact and changed my perspective on life altogether. I can see in retrospect that although I was high on acid, the agent that was working was not the LSD, but God Himself, in spite of the drug.

There are professionals and religious people that advise not talking to a person about the Good News of Jesus Christ when they are high, stoned, or drunk, on drugs or alcohol. They will say, "You are only talking to the alcohol or the drug. You can't reach the person." The Bible says: *"So shall My word be that goes forth out of My mouth: it shall not return to Me void [without producing any effect, useless], but it shall accomplish that which I please and purpose, and it shall prosper in the thing for which I sent it."(Isaiah 55:11 Amplified)* So why would anyone assume that the alcohol or drugs are stronger than the Word of God? I can attest from my personal experience that God is indeed stronger than the drugs and alcohol and He speaks to us right where we are and He is not limited in any way!

As had been my practice, I went to San Francisco to buy Acid with the intent of 'distributing' it in Laguna Beach and making a little money. I went to hear Big Brother and the Holding Company at the Straight Theater on Haight Street and someone came up to me and told me to open my mouth. He put a #5 Cap in it; I swallowed, then someone else came up and repeated the ritual. As it turns out, these two caps were some of the cleanest acid I have ever taken. The next day, I went to an upstairs flat, where I heard they were selling, and bought $1200 worth of the acid. It was a light pink powder, and was purportedly from Czechoslovakia, and man, it was smooth and good.

When I got back to Laguna Beach I took some of my new find over to my good friend Steve's 'pad' so he and his girlfriend Karen and I could drop together. We smoked a joint of pot and then they went in the kitchen, (the only other room in the place), purportedly to pop rice. They explained that it would be like popcorn (except that it didn't look like or taste like it when it was done). While they were popping rice in the kitchen, I went ahead and dropped some acid and lay back on the mattress and started to relax. Soon, I was watching paisley patterns with bold black outlines slowly float across the wall. Then, quite abruptly my vision focused on one black edge and it was as though my eyes had a zoom lens: the edge of the paisley filled my vision in less than a heart beat. Within a nanosecond, everything went to a shimmering curtain of Gold and simultaneously I felt a stab of fear and awe in the center of my being. It was only for a fraction of a second, but it was probably all I could bear and in that amount of time, I knew something that could not be communicated or described even in volumes: I had seen the place where God lives! How did I know this? I don't know, but it was one of those sensations where I would have to say that I know that I know that I know, and that's that. The experience left me completely and keenly alert and it also left me with an unshakable sense of awe and an awareness of the Presence of God!

One of the peculiar aspects about this experience was that I saw God's Presence as being wrapped in gold and splendor. The friends that I associated with in those days usually talked about the clear white light of eastern mysticism and for a long time I wondered why God didn't show up like that, with the clear white light. Today, I realize that the one true God Almighty's presence is represented by gold and God introduced me to Himself as He is in truth, not as the white light of mysticism, which is not really Him. He wanted me to **know** Him, He sought me out, I didn't find Him—I was seeking and the method I was using was mysticism, but He was doing the finding. He reached right into my world at my point of need; that's what He does. Now, don't get me wrong, I did not become a Christian at this time. That nanosecond of experience was all I could take at that point and it was several years more before I could accept the Word of Salvation from the Bible.

This experience was HUGE for me in that now I had faith in God! I never again talked about whether or not God existed; I knew He was real. I sometimes had questions about His nature, but never about His existence. Please, do not think that God cannot speak to anyone because of his or her state of mind! I have heard pastors say one can't talk to someone when they are drunk. Don't believe it! I believe these people are looking at the situation out of their own intellect and not from the perspective of the Bible or with the assistance of the Lord and the Holy Spirit. We just need to be filled with His Spirit and speak His Word and it will not return to Him void.

"So shall My word be that goes forth out of My mouth: it shall not return to Me void [without producing any effect, useless], but it shall accomplish that which I please and purpose, and it shall prosper in the thing for which I sent it." Isaiah 55:11 Amplified

"Surely the arm of the Lord is not too short to save, nor his ear too dull to hear." Isaiah 59:1

CHAPTER 6

CLARKSTON

Clarkston, Washington is a little town that sits right on the Idaho/Washington border; running parallel with the border is the Snake River and just across, is Clarkston's sister city, Lewiston, Idaho. Only the river and two state governments separate them, but they are joined at the hip by a two-lane bridge and the US historical legacy of their respective city names. Lewiston and Clarkston were named after Meriwether Lewis and William Clark from the infamous Corps of Discovery expedition of the Jeffersonian era. Lewis and Clark land marked this territory on their way to the continent's western coast and the area still radiates the deep historical ramifications. The twin towns are neighbored by the Nez Perce Indian Reservation. The past seems so close in this part of the world; visions of explorers, Indians and US cavalry are easily conjured as if it was only yesterday.

For the last one hundred-plus years the Clarkston/Lewiston area has been, and still is, primarily a farm support and pulp mill community. The community is surrounded for miles upon miles with nothing but dirt; dirt that is producing crops a majority of the year. So the town is comprised primarily of farmers and vendors who support the farmers and those who are related in some way to the farmers... and then of course the local Indians and cowboys. As is true across the country, the farmers are the heartland and backbone of the country. The combination of its agricultural heritage as well as being a significant historical piece of America's westward exploration and expansion makes this relatively small part of the country a very solid, conservative specimen of Americana. Stand anywhere in the surrounding area and take a deep breath; the hint of dust lingers in the air and with it a feeling that this area and its values are solid: yes, these are our roots as a nation; this is what is right with the world.

During the late '60's the country was still fighting the war in Vietnam to combat the domino effect of toppling governments to the communists' aggression in Southeast Asia (or was it for first dibs for the tungsten and rubber? Hmm...). Dissatisfaction with political agendas brought in a wave of colliding ideology and along with it the youth's rejection of the status quo hypocrisy. Out of it all sprang a counterculture and the Hippie Movement-- the Peace, Love, and Granola-Tea movement as I call it.

Espousing the hippie lifestyle and the Peace, Love, and Granola Tea ideology was a natural progression for me. I had rejected the lifestyle of my father, with the corporate car, double martini's after work, and a house in the tract developments. He didn't look very happy to me, and there had to be more to life than this waiting for me as I grew old, so no thanks, you can keep the golden ticket if that's what it looked like. I decided living back to nature; back to the earth must be a better way. At the same time, I was still searching for the 'God answer'. It wasn't really a conscious thing, but there was a gnawing hunger deep within my being that the answer was out there and I wanted to find it. I had been introduced to psychedelics through the Mystic Arts World influence in Laguna Beach, a Timothy Leary spin-off, and looked to psychedelic and hallucinogenic drugs to bring me spiritual awakening. To make a few bucks I dabbled in dealing those drugs very briefly. However, Mafia kingpins and drug lords were starting to take over the drug peddling business from the Mystic Arts World affiliates and people were showing up dead with their arms cut off. I had a brush with the Mafia in Laguna Beach, where they used some strong-arm tactics to try to 'recruit' me into doing some 'distribution' for them, from which I narrowly escaped and quickly decided this wasn't my scene. I got out. I still partook with friends, but I left San Francisco, Laguna Beach, and dealing behind.

  We lived in Lewiston briefly, ironically on Normal Hill, one block down from a little church that had a neon sign that read: "Old Time Gospel" out front. Our little apartment and the church were on Second Street, on Normal Hill in Lewiston, Idaho. Some evenings I sat in our little apartment and got really nervous or agitated and I smoked a little weed to calm down. On two such occasions it occurred on Tuesday evening when the church was alive with activity and music. I walked down the street as if drawn to the church. Twice, I stood out front of the church listening to the noises coming from inside and heard boisterous "Praise the Lord!" and joyful, exuberant music. I liked the Old Time Gospel sign. I was getting tired of the modern era. Much had been tried and done. It had become apparent that the Love and Peace to the World generation had gone over to lust and what piece of the world do you want? I had an intense desire to go inside the little church, but I always came up with some lame excuse to give myself as to why not. It would take another act of God to get me inside.

By the time my wife, new baby, and I moved into our little one bedroom $50.00 per month rental house on Second Street in Clarkston, we were the quintessential long-haired hippies, living off my unemployment insurance and then welfare, making our own beer and wine off government food stamp commodities, rolling our own cigarettes, making our own bread, and growing and partaking of marijuana. I was a lanky 6'4" with long, wavy strawberry blonde hair and a flaming red full beard. It would be an understatement to say that we stood out as we walked downtown in this conservative community! There may have been a small percentage of other residents that espoused a similar lifestyle to mine, but a red-headed, hot tempered, high tripping hippie with a penchant for attracting trouble and attention—now there's a rare commodity! Funny thing was that I thought I was fairly low-key, easy-going and that life as it existed at the time was the norm for me. I had no idea that life could be any different.

PEA-ING

I didn't work much during this time in my life except for the summer I drove pea combine for the wet peas and I think it was this experience that taught me to actually work a full day's labor. I peddled my bicycle up the roughly two-mile trek to the plateau and joined the other harvesters who all arrived at the Field Shop in the Lewiston Orchards (which was really no longer an orchard, but a housing development) in time to get to the field at 7:00 am. The first field of the season was right next to the shop and as the season progressed, the ripe fields crept closer and closer to Grangeville up on the prairie. It was an hour just to get to the field, and an hour to get back to Lewiston--without traffic! Traffic congestion on the prairies of Idaho was a tractor moving at a snail's pace and refusing to pull over, but that rarely happened, as the Idahoans look out for each other. All the farm boys who were harvesting agreed pea-ing was good money. I was at first perplexed as to why they thought $2.30 per hour, which was a little more than minimum wage at that time, was good money. But I learned what they meant as time went on. We worked long days and got home too tired to party and when pea harvesting was done, that money lasted almost all winter! So from sun up to sun down during the long days of summer, I sat on a pea combine and the only company I had was the soft whirring of the combine as it collected the peas and my own thoughts. From this time comes what my family now calls, The Pea Song, which is my lyrics, put to the tune of "I Still Miss Someone" by Johnny Cash. Over the years I have created a plethora of impromptu songs birthed from the emotions of the moment and I belt them out with gusto, but as easily as they come with effervescence, they dissolve from memory like soda water fizz, but the Pea Song has endured through the years. The other thing that came from those long lonely days of combining was a reckoning with me as I took in the beautiful rolling hills with the crops swaying in the wind and felt the wind against my sun-parched cheeks. Although I can't say I derived inner peace from the solitude, I grew accustomed to my own company.

"Be still and know that I am God; I will be exalted among the nations, I will be exalted in the earth" Psalm 46:10

PENANCE

I spent a Lenten season going to the Catholic Church, and praying a lot of Our Fathers for the sins that I had committed. I didn't pray these because the priest in the confessional told me to, but because I thought I needed to atone for my sins in order to get into heaven. When I first went back to the Catholic Church I had lived more than a decade in hippie-dom, so I dutifully went to confession and told the priest a quick synopsis of my sins. Of course I anticipated needing to stay for hours to recite all the prayers that I expected him to lay on me, but the strangest thing happened: from the other side of the screen, I heard him gulp and then he told me to say a prayer for him! That was it! Today when I think of him I say a prayer for him. I don't exactly know why I quit going to the Catholic Church, however I do remember praying and thinking that I had said an awful lot of prayers. I told the Father, that if I ever said enough prayers to get me to heaven, then would He please apply my extra prayers to someone's account so that they could get to heaven too. Then I began to think about the idea of penance getting one to heaven, and I began to realize that there was no way of knowing if I was even ever going to get to heaven. What measure of sin was outweighed by what measure of prayer?

"For it is by grace you have been saved, through faith—and this not from yourselves, it is the gift of God—not by works, so that no one can boast." Ephesians 2: 8,9

"And everyone who calls on the name of the Lord will be saved." Acts 2:21

Chapter 7

Phyllis and Dennis

A few doors down from us in Clarkston, on the opposite side of the street lived Dennis and Phyllis Delp and their 5 children. Dennis and Phyllis were Christians. Although I don't recall either of them frequenting a church, they were true believers and Phyllis was a praying woman. She has recounted in recent years her vivid memories of the first time she saw us, just after we moved into the little one bedroom rental. She was sitting on her front porch talking to her kids as my wife and I walked down the street, pulling baby Jennifer in a wagon. My wife was wearing shorts, a see-through top, and boots. I was wearing shorts and boots, had long hair and a flaming red beard. Phyllis recounts that she prayed, "Oh Lord, don't let those people come over here. But, if they need me send them over." She was surprised at how fast we whipped that wagon around and came directly to her house to meet her! I have no doubt that Phyllis was a significant spiritual influence in my life. I used to say that I was sure that Phyllis whipped a prayer on me. In our eyes, she was definitely an instrument of God's love. Phyllis and Dennis didn't put on airs or get judgmental with us, or get religious. They were simple people with good hearts: hard-working, generous, and loving. From my perspective, God uses the most humble to spread His love and the Word of His Love. We were always welcome at the Delp household; there was always a cup of coffee and conversation available for any guest. I remember one time when the coffee grounds had to be used more than once for lack of funds, but whatever they had they always shared.

My friend Dennis Delp helped me get a part time job at Pacific Hide and Fur, a scrap metal recycling yard, where I broke batteries. Pacific Hide and Fur had no doubt transitioned its business focus over the decades to change with the times, as so many businesses have to do to remain a viable enterprise. They went from a company that tanned and processed pelts and hides to a metal recycling plant. One of the metals PH&F recycled was lead from old batteries. Since the rubber shell was no good for their recycling efforts the lead and the rubber had to be separated. For this purpose they had built a machine that was a slower, hydraulic-driven version of the French Guillotine that took off Marie Antoinette and King Louis XVI's heads. This blade was not as sharp and was driven by an old gasoline lawnmower motor but the force was great enough to take off the top of any battery that came in, including huge truck and tractor batteries.

Dennis told me a couple of incidents in his life that helped to confirm and gel my faith in God. For most of his adult life he worked at Pacific Hide and Fur sorting and cutting metals into easily transportable sizes for the recycling process. One day a truck brought a massive shaft of steel. The boss weighed it, and the crane off-loaded it from the truck, but 'Boss' couldn't figure out what to do with it as it was too large to put on the rail cars, and the cutting torches were only good for less than an eight inch thickness of steel. These torches used oxygen and propane for the cutting; basically like oxygen and acetylene cutting torches however the propane doesn't cut as neatly as acetylene, but is a lot cheaper. So the huge shaft of steel sat on the ground for days while they contemplated what to do. Now, Dennis was not a well-educated man, but he had an uncanny ability to size up the construction, shape, weight, and composition of a metallic object and pretty well determine what needed to be done to it to accomplish a said task. I am convinced that he had a level of genius that psychologists do not acknowledge or perhaps even have the wherewithal to measure. After cogitating on it a couple of days, Dennis went to Boss and said, "I can cut it." Boss said, "Do it!" And so he did. His innate understanding of his job made him realize that the shaft was hollow and not solid as it appeared, so he didn't have to cut through feet of metal but only about six inches. He proceeded to cut this enormous rod of steel down to size with a torch and a technique that I could not hope to duplicate even with the experience of years! With little education and little time, he had solved the complex problem that I defy engineers to duplicate. I had always esteemed intellect as being of premium importance and I was amazed to meet this humble man whom God had gifted to do engineering feats. It was my first glimpse at seeing that not only those with high I Q's and education are well endowed—the lucky ones, so to speak--but God has given all of us specific gifting and that when we honor the gifting within us, we do amazing feats that boggle the mind.

"We have different gifts, according to the grace given us. If a man's gift is prophesying, let him use it in proportion to his faith". Romans 12:6

Another time in the Metal Yard Dennis walked across the yard holding a two-inch diameter steel pin from a Caterpillar tractor. He was having serious doubts about the existence of God due to some struggles in life he was experiencing, so as he walked Dennis asked in his heart: "Lord, if you're real, show me." At that moment the pin separated into two pieces. Dennis was astounded! He thoroughly examined the steel, looking for evidence of previous weakness or fracturing. It just broke!! To most people this breakage would mean nothing, and certainly not be proof confirmation from God of His existence, but Dennis knew steel better than most men know their wives. He worked with it, he was involved with it every day; he knew its shortcomings and strengths, so to him this was significant. Isn't it interesting how the Almighty God took a breaking of a two-inch diameter pin to speak volumes to this man and it eradicated his doubting. As Dennis relayed this story to me, I could see the look of astonishment in his eyes. It was a life-changing moment for him and in hearing the story; it built up my faith as well. God knew and He used exactly what would speak most effectively to this Metal Man.

"Do you not know? Have you not heard? The Lord is the everlasting God, the Creator of the ends of the earth. He will not grow tired or weary, and his understanding no one can fathom. He gives strength to the weary, and increases the power of the weak. Even youths grow tired and weary, and young men stumble and fall; but those who hope in the Lord will renew their strength. They will soar on wings like eagles; they will run and not grow weary, they will walk and not be faint." Isaiah 40: 28-31

One time Phyllis whipped a prayer on a family of bats that took up residence in the upper story of their house. Dennis tried a few things to rid the house of the bats, but none of them worked. I asked if the bats were harming anything and she answered in the negative, but her concern was that her house was a Christian house, and bats were associated with witches and other forces of darkness. Phyllis prayed that the bats leave her house and find a different place to reside. Sometime later as I was walking down the street, I saw and heard bats going into the cracks of a telephone pole. I was astounded that they fit in there! Sure enough, the bats in the Delp's house had gone and had found a new place. Upon hearing that I had seen the bats in the telephone pole, Phyllis was relieved they had found sufficient accommodations.

"The prayer of a righteous [woman] is powerful and effective."
James 5:16b

CHAPTER 8

THE GARDEN

During this time, I met a guy named Frank, an employee for some Economic Development branch of the feds. I don't know why exactly he wanted to help me, but I guess Frank was a great guy who wanted to help people. Frank was very instrumental in acquiring a piece of land that I could borrow to raise a few vegetables. He talked a single lady into letting us use her vacant 1.5 acres for the summer. The whole lot was covered in weeds, with a collapsing, unused chicken shed on the back part of the lot. Some old rusted out water lines ran up the west side of the lot for about one hundred and fifty feet. We repaired the water lines so that we could irrigate at least the lower part. Frank rented a tractor to plow under the weeds, and with a little bit of hoeing and planting; we had an organic produce garden. I planted a variety of vegetables and fruit: zucchini, tomatoes, cantaloupe, corn--and a little substance some people refer to as Mary Jane. A local boy had given me seeds that he said was really righteous (strong) pot. Indeed, when it sprouted there was a red streak that went up the shoots, which indicated it was going to be 'righteous' all right-- and I can attest to the fact that it was! I grew some terrific fruits and vegetables that year. My tomatoes thrived and I had a bumper crop. They were really great tomatoes and they were organically grown, but had the protection of the Lord. You see, I didn't know the Lord at this point, but as I planted each seed, I said an "Our Father". I figured it couldn't hurt. I never had to worry about insects and bugs eating my crop. My neighbor had a garden too, however his tomatoes were eaten by tomato worms, but not a one of my tomatoes was touched!

I planted the marijuana in between the stalks of corn, as I had heard through the hippie scuttlebutt this was the way to do it. The corn grew faster and taller than the pot and therefore successfully hid it from sight. I don't think Frank ever knew that the Feds were subsidizing marijuana growth, but they sure were! God Bless the Feds! I have come to realize since then that an important truth was at play in that garden: God's principles work— even for the ungodly. He is not a respecter of persons. He does not show partiality.

"Then Peter began to speak: "I now realize how true it is that God does not show favoritism but accepts men from every nation who fear him and do what is right." Acts 10:34,35

"For God does not show favoritism." Romans 2:22

Chapter 9

The Chief

One Saturday, as I was weeding in the garden and was standing among the rows of corn, the Clarkston Police Chief, Chief Tilton, with his wife and his two kids road by on their bicycles. Chief Tilton waved and said, "Hi Tim, how's the corn doing?" With my feet brushing against the new marijuana shoots, I waved back and replied, "Oh, just fine, Chief." Now one might inquire as to how the chief knew my name. The Chief and I knew each other-- it's not that we went out for coffee or had lunch together, but you might say we had a history!

There had been at least two incidents that caused my path to cross the chief's (close encounters of the police kind) and definitely others that made him aware of me. The first time was after I had spent the night in his jail. The evening before I had gone into Lewiston and was already somewhat inebriated, however, once there I went into the liquor store a bought a pint of liquor. After some more drinking, I decided to cross the main drag through town. This doesn't sound like a big feat, however it can be a bit tricky once the alcohol has had its full effect. I was drunk as a skunk as I went to the corner at the signal light, but I didn't wait for the light to turn green. Cars were screeching to a halt as I staggered my way across the intersection. The Lewiston cops soon saw what was going on, and threw me in jail out of protection for the motorists and myself. They charged me with possession of an open bottle, detained me four hours to let me sober up, harassed me a bit, and then let my wife make my bail.

    Liquor was sold later in Washington than in Idaho, so I went back over the river to Clarkston. Even though it was getting late, I detoured my way home and landed at a bar down by the river. This section of town doesn't exist anymore because it has been flooded by the building of the Little Goose dam, but prior to that it was the most happening place in Clarkston-- especially after one AM when they quit selling in Idaho. At this bar I met a guy named Big Jim. Big Jim, an American Indian, was up from Arizona attending a wake on the Nez Perce Indian Reservation and we became drinking buddies for the night. When the bar shut down for the night, we went to my house, but it wasn't Party City, so Jim suggested we go to Lapwai to party. Lapwai was on the 'res' and because he knew people there, we were bound to have a good time. We piled into his car and headed East to Lapwai... or so I thought. In actuality we were headed southwest, on a diagonal street through Clarkston when the police stopped us. Jim was really drunk and therefore was headed the wrong way. I must have been really drunk to even get into a car with someone as drunk as he was! The cops determined that we were both too drunk to drive, so they told us to go to my house and sleep it off. But oh no, not Jim! He was now determined to go party in Lapwai, so we waited until the cops left and got back in the car. Had Jim driven correctly toward Lapwai we might have escaped being detected by the cops, since it was only a few blocks to the bridge, out of Washington and into Idaho. But once again he went the wrong way! This time we headed south through downtown Clarkston. The same cops saw us, stopped us, and arrested us this time. When they declared we were under arrest, I thought it was a joke and started to walk off, but was quickly detained by one of the cops and both of us were charged with being drunk in public. Their police report had a trumped-up story about how I was fighting and kicking Jim and had him pinned down on the ground. What a crock!! The next morning when they brought us a TV dinner for breakfast, I refused to eat. Prior to this night, I had made a decision that if I ever got put in jail, I wouldn't eat, based on my belief, even before knowing the Biblical stance on it, that there is power in fasting. Chief Tilton tried to get me to eat the breakfast. It was clear from his face that he didn't know what to do with a prisoner that refused to eat. I would love to have the Chief as an opponent in a poker game because what he was thinking and feeling was written all over his face and it was apparent that I was an anomaly to him. While Jim was eating we talked about the charges that were against us. I asked him if he remembered us being in a fight.

He said that he didn't remember anything, but that his head hurt. Both cops corroborated so Big Jim and I were found guilty based on their report. Evidently there is still an ongoing emotional feud between some cowboys and some Indians, so I presume the court authorities brushed our case off as just another incident between the Whites and the Indians.

One later incident that supports this idea happened late one afternoon when two cowboys from up on the flats came to my house, and invited me to go with them to North Lewiston to get drunk and get into a fight with some Indians. I have never figured out why they wanted a longhair to go with them, since I couldn't punch my way out of a paper bag, but off we went to a cowboy bar. I don't think they ever found that fight they were looking for that night, but some how I got into an arm turning contest with an Indian fellow. I knew that I couldn't win since I hadn't done any physical work for years, however I had read that the trick of winning an arm wrestling match is to just hold off the opponent until he gets tired. While I was struggling to hold my own, a little guy came up to the table and socked me in the jaw with his fist! I put my left hand up with my palm facing the pugilist and an onlooker shouted, "Spoken like an Indian!" I later found out that the guy who punched me was a professional boxer. I soon lost the arm turning match. Much later in the evening, I ran across the boxer again and he had his hand bandaged up and when he removed the bandage he revealed a split in his hand where he had struck me. I invited him to my house and offered to stitch him up as I had made some suture needles in case my wife tore when she delivered our second child in natural at-home childbirth. Unfortunately the solution that I had stored the needles in had too high of a water content and the needles had become rusty, so we had a drink and he left.

These stories are just a sprinkling of some of the events happening in my life in Clarkston, but from them it is apparent I had a history and a record with the small town and that I indeed had a penchant for the rough and rowdy side of life. In addition there were other issues, some might call confrontational. Some time before the chief and his family biked by the garden, I was sitting at home drinking some of my home brew beer (that stuff was stout; the weakest was 6% alcohol, and the double-fermented versions had an alcohol content of about 12%.), getting a little drunk, and two of my beer drinking buddies came in and said the cops had just raided 'the house.' The House, located several blocks south of us, was a big house used as a low-rent boarding house for young people and it had a rep for drug trafficking. I had a friend or two that lived in 'The House' and when Chief Tilton busted it, I was incensed! I rallied my two drinking buddies and the three of us walked down to the 'cop shop'. We walked up and down in front of the station with its four jail cells, assuming our picketing stance, but without the signs. It didn't take long for us to get the attention of the Chief of Police and he stuck his head out a window and asked me by name what I wanted. We talked a little and I demanded he let my buddy John and the others go and eventually he agreed to let John go.

John was the only one arrested that came over to my house and drank with me—that made him my friend, so I was satisfied.

Although these stories do not directly relate with how the Lord was working in my life, they do paint a fairly accurate picture of how my life was tumultuous and chaotic in many ways at this time. It was fairly significant that I had been arrested and booked for drunkenness in that up until this time, I had done many things with far more serious legal ramifications without being caught. On numerous occasions, I had emerged unscathed from car searches with drugs discreetly tucked on board. One time the cops actually found a stash of pot and confiscated it, but didn't prosecute. Why? I don't know exactly, but it seemed I had the greased pig syndrome as far as the law was concerned, but luck doesn't run forever. In retrospect, perhaps it was God's mercy that I got caught on a relatively minor charge.

Chapter 10

THE COFFEE HOUSE

During these tumultuous months the Lord continued drawing me toward Himself in little ways, here and there. One day as I was walking downtown (I walked everywhere since we espoused the hippie lifestyle and didn't believe in using cars for transportation) a young girl whom I was only cursorily acquainted with asked if I had been to the new coffee house on Main Street in Lewiston, located in the basement of the building where a Head Shop (a shop that sells drug-related paraphernalia) had been. I responded with a no but she said it was free, and I had plenty of time on my hands, so I went to check it out one afternoon. As I entered the room the aroma of overcooked, stale coffee hit my nostrils with ballistic force. It was brewing in one of those aluminum brew pots that held at least a gallon and continued to cook the coffee for hours until it resembled sludge and had enough bitterness to contort the face of even the stoutest coffee drinker. The sparsely furnished room contained a simple table with some chairs and an old worn out davenport.

Stories of a Salvation

There were only three guys occupying the coffeehouse and they were reading, not even talking. I was about to turn and leave, when one of them, presumably the leader and certainly the elder, spoke. I kind of remember him as being rather homely- looking, while the other two just looked like kids in their late teens or early twenties.

The leader asked me to sit down and offered me a cup of coffee. I accepted, and found it equaled its pungent aroma! Then he started telling me the salvation message, I think! It went totally over my head, but nevertheless I thank God that he was brave enough to do it! When he finished, he asked if I wanted to accept Jesus as my Lord. I said no, I wanted to go home and clean up my act first. He let out a sigh that I can hear today!! I had missed the entire point of the work that Jesus had done on the cross: in that He paid the price for me when I was unlovely and screwed up, and there was no way to make myself more presentable to Him than I was at that point!! Nevertheless, this guy had read the Word of God to me and God's Word takes hold and does not return to Him without having an effect.

"For as the rain and snow come down from the heavens, and return not there again, but water the earth and make it bring forth and sprout, that it may give seed to the sower and bread to the eater, So shall My word be that goes forth out of My mouth: it shall not return to Me void [without producing any effect, useless], but it shall accomplish that which I please and purpose, and it shall prosper in the thing for which I sent it."
Isa 55:10-11, Amplified

Chapter 11

Two Ladies

Sometime later, I was walking to the grocery store, and as I entered I saw a poster on the window that proclaimed: "The Maharishi Mahesh Yogi will teach you to meditate". I looked at the sign and a prayer went up from my heart. It went something like this: "God I know that I need you, and maybe these are the people You would have tell me about you. But, I have heard about these people, they come with their hand out for money first and then they will teach me to meditate. That just doesn't sound like you to me. I could travel and search the world over and never find the right people, so God, you send to my house the people you want to teach me about you."

I quickly forgot the prayer; in fact, I don't think that I even consciously realized that I had said one. So of course the next thing that happened was that one of the canvassing cults, like the Mormons or the Jehovah's Witnesses came to our door, right? Not so! Short time later two ladies came and knocked on the door. They related that as they were driving down the street, God told them to come to our house. They didn't go to the house on either side of us nor did they go to any house on the other side of the street, they only came to our house. They went on to say that God told them to tell us about Jesus Christ and the Holy Ghost. It turns out that they attended that little church down the street from where we used to live on Normal Hill in Lewiston, the one with the neon sign that read "Old Time Gospel". I mean, this was a very small church, there couldn't have been more than 75 adults in the whole church, but 2 of them were driving by my house in the neighboring town and picked my house to stop and tell us about Jesus! What are the odds! Well, those are the odds we get with God.

    I have to admit; I had completely forgotten my heart prayer and did not want to be bothered, so I told them to talk with my wife. Afterwards, my wife said she wanted to go to church and become a Christian! I told her I would go with her, so they didn't fill her head with any funny ideas, so I finally stepped foot in that Old Time Gospel church!

"...if we are faithless, he will remain faithful..." II Timothy 2:13

Chapter 12

The Holy Ghost

We went to the church that had the Old Time Gospel sign displayed where I had previously paced up and down on the sidewalk out front, stoned. It was filled with the Holy Ghost and Peter Shebly was the pastor, although we all called him Brother Shebly because of his or her conviction that all of us are equal in the Lord and no one deserves a specific title. I passed many spiritual milestones while going to this little "full gospel" church. I accepted Jesus Christ as my savior--although it was not in a church service-- on my bed at home. (I have always suspected that it was while Phyllis Delp was praying for me). The church was really adamant about getting baptized in water in the name of Jesus. They felt that this was so important that if someone called up the pastor, he called the church members for a baptism at that very moment. One day my wife decided that she wanted to get baptized so she called Brother Shebly and he contacted as many as he could and everyone went down to the boat launch to view the baptism in the cold Snake River.

She was immersed in the water, but did not come up speaking in tongues as the church wanted and expected, but that was cool with me. I decided since it was getting toward fall, and I was planning to get baptized later, it might as well be sooner than later because later meant colder when it came to the Snake River!

Although, I was saved and filled with the Holy Ghost, not all the bad stuff left right away. One day, in the afternoon, I got into an argument with my wife. At that time I had some homegrown pot that was really potent, two tokes was all it took to get into the ozone. I had grown this pot in my garden, but the harvest was small since I had to harvest it early when someone started to pick the bottom leaves. Once one person in the valley knew about the pot growing in my corn patch, the next time the Chief came by the garden, it probably wouldn't be to ask how the corn was growing. Even though I was saved, I wasn't set free yet. After the argument, I took a little of the two toke red, and toked up. I wandered around the valley for a while. But when evening church started, I was there, high as a kite. The church always said that God was in control of the services and I was to do whatever God wanted me to do, so I did. During the singing, I shouted, "Brother Shebly, I need prayer!" Immediately all the men formed a circle around me while I kneeled at my chair. As they prayed, I felt the Lord say; "I am going to deliver you from marijuana." I thought, "ok. Now what?" I looked up, since I was on my knees, and someone looked at me and said, "Praise the Lord!" So I said, "Praise the Lord." All the men left and returned to their seats, or the stage, as the case may be. I sat quietly for a moment, and then I thought, "What should I do with this can of pot in my pocket?" I still had a Prince Albert can that was half full of two-toke red homegrown. I felt that the Lord said, "Go ask Brother Shebly." Brother Shebly had been sitting toward the back of the church during the singing, so I went over and said, "The lord has just delivered me from Marijuana, and told me to ask you what I was supposed to do with this. His jaw dropped and his eyes widened and he said, "Go throw it in the river!"

 The Snake River Bridge was about four blocks from the church; I turned on my heel and left the service that very moment, walked to the middle of the bridge, and threw the can and its contents into the river. That wasn't the end of the deliverance, however. The next day I went to Brother Shebly's house for a visit and as I was walking down Prospect Hill toward home, a car started honking its horn about a block back. As it came along side where I was walking, and I could assess it was in real good shape for a car from the forties. The driver was a guy that was younger than I, and he had two young, cute girls with him. I got in, thinking that I could get a ride home. They started talking about going to Lewiston to party, even though this was the middle of the day. One of the girls had a bottle of Mateus wine, which I had recently heard was supposed to be very good. The guy lit a joint, and passed it to the girl to his right; she took a toke and passed it to the girl on her right, who took a toke and passed it to me. "How strange", I thought that

I had never seen any of them before, and I never found out their names. When the toke got to me I thought, "Oh, just a little toke won't hurt". But it was out! God has grace. I gave it back to the guy, he re-lit it and the toke went to each of the girls again. When it got to me, it was out again. God has mercy. I gave it to the guy one more time, saying, "It's out again." He re-lit it and we went through the ritual passing of the joint one more time. This time I realized that I needed to make a decision. I said, "I don't know why I am doing this. God delivered me from this stuff last night in church." I gave it to the girl next to me. The driver stopped that car faster than a blink and the ride was over just like that! I walked the rest of the way home. Whom Jesus sets free is free indeed.

Jesus said: "So if the Son sets you free, you will be free indeed." John 8:36

But the most significant teaching of Brother Shebly that took hold in my life still resounds with me today: the Bible is the Standard by which we live and it is vital to go to a Bible-teaching church. Whatever is taught must line up with the Bible, if it doesn't, spit it out. And the church must be filled with the Spirit of God; if His Spirit leaves, then I am to leave also.

Although I gained much from going to this little church, it did seem to have some funny ideas. The women only wore dresses, never pants and they let their hair grow long, always rolling it up on top of their heads (unless the Holy ghost came upon them, then their hair came down and their heads shook and the hair flowed down in long waves). They made many rules out of things they had read in the Bible such as women not cutting their hair or wearing expensive jewelry. They went so far as to say that if you didn't speak with other tongues, they didn't know whether you were saved. Early on, I was instructed that I needed to "tarry for the Holy Ghost", so I stayed at the alter to pray and praise God for a length of time after service, waiting for God to give me the ability to speak in an unknown prayer language. In those days I had a lot of free time on my hands, so it wasn't an inconvenience to stay. Someone suggested perhaps I should cut my hair to receive the Holy Ghost and pray in other tongues and they had some scripture contorted to fit their claim. But this sounded like hooey to me, so I didn't cut my hair and I began to speak in tongues and received the Holy Ghost. It didn't seem that God cared if I had long hair, or smoked pot for that matter. He had seen me at my 'lowlife' stages and had compassion on me. He met me at my point (or in my case, points) of need and He accepted me as I was. He didn't look at the outside of a person and He didn't condemn me. Not only did He not condemn me, but He had a plan to bring me out of my personal hell and to reinstate me as what He had created me to be in the first place: a man, created in His image, to have dominion, life abundant, and deliverance from my problems on this earth.

    The religious trappings and rules, I rejected. They were not who God is and He did not advocate religiosity. In fact, it was the religious leaders of His day that He came down on and called them a den of vipers. I imagine it was hard to "feel the love" in that conversation. Over the years I have gone to many churches, and left. But Brother Shebly was the only one that ever came to me after I left and asked why I left. I can still see Brother Shebly today as he sat in my front room and he bowed his head when I told him that I had left because the anointing had left.

"God said, Let Us [Father, Son, and Holy Spirit] make mankind in Our image, after Our likeness, and let them have complete authority over the fish of the sea, the birds of the air, the [tame] beasts, and over all of the earth, and over everything that creeps upon the earth. So God created man in His own image, in the image and likeness of God He created him: male and female He created them. And God blessed them and said to them, Be fruitful, multiply, and fill the earth, and subdue it [using all its vast resources in the service of God and man]; and have dominion over the fish of the sea, the birds of the air, and over every living creature that moves upon the earth." Genesis 1:26-28

"Every Scripture is God-breathed (given by His inspiration) and profitable for instruction, for reproof and conviction of sin, for correction of error and discipline in obedience, [and] for training in righteousness (in holy living, in conformity to God's will in thought, purpose, and action), so that the man of God many be complete and proficient, well fitted and thoroughly equipped for every good work." II Timothy 3:16,17

Chapter 13

T.M. AND THE DOGS

In the Sixties and early Seventies Transcendental Meditation was making strides into America. When it was first introduced in the States the organization claimed to be a religion and they promoted it as such. Gradually the proponents of TM found that they could get into public schools by promoting TM as a meditative technique rather than a religion. After all they were only teaching a technique, not proselytizing a religion.

I had some friends that had delved into TM and their report to me was that they gave a flower, a fruit and a hundred dollars, for which they were given a mantra. A Mantra was a Sanskrit word that they were supposed to repeat over and over, thereby bringing peace of mind or whatever was desired. One of my Clarkston friends in particular, Jay, came over one day excited about the demonstrable "proof" that TM worked. Jay relayed an experience he had at a TM meeting where one of the TM'ers started to meditate and a dog in the room came over to where he was meditating. He went on to explain that according to the meeting leader, the dog sensed the peace of the meditator and gravitated to that peace. It was an interesting idea, but was never demonstrated to me and what came out of it actually was a demonstration of the power of the Almighty God and His love and concern for us, His children, more specifically, me, His new child.

When my faith in Jesus Christ was young and fragile, when it was new and needed protection, when it was possible to question the singularity of the gospel as the means of salvation that is when God the Father stepped in to reaffirm my decision to follow Him. As a farmer or gardener will take steps to protect a young sapling by tying it to a firmly grounded stake or as a protective tube might be placed to surround a seedling to shelter it from the elements, so God will protect His children. A few days after Jay's TM testimonial, I was walking the five blocks from downtown to my little one bedroom house, when I glanced behind me and saw to my astonishment, a pack of about fifteen to twenty dogs following me on the sidewalk! They were various sizes, shapes and colors; some were breeds and some were "Heinz 57" Mongrels and they must have come from every home in the neighborhood. As I walked they continued to follow behind! If I stopped, they stopped. It wasn't as though they were trying to attack me as a pack of wild dogs or wolves would; it seemed they just wanted to follow me. I have never been a dog-lover by nature and this experience has not happened before or since in my life; and at the time, it had me wondering. As I got close to our little rental house I turned around to see if perhaps they had wandered off or gone on their merry way, as I hadn't given them any encouragement whatsoever. But no, they were still there! "What was I going to do with that many dogs?" I thought. Our house was way too small. I shouted at the dogs to shoo, but to no avail. I threw a rock at them. Then and only then did they disperse and leave, dogs trotting off in all directions.

    The point that was most incredible to me was that I wasn't meditating or praying or doing anything of the sort at that time. There was nothing that I was doing except walking home. The truth that rang true to me in this bizarre little episode was that God the Father, whom I had given my heart to, was infinitely more powerful than a technique such as Transcendental Meditation and He cared enough for me to demonstrate His love and His power to me. Just to me.

" Be still, and know that I am God: I will be exalted among the heathen, I will be exalted in the earth." Ps 46:10 **KJV**

    Since these events I have learned the Biblical perspective on meditation. As Christians we are encouraged to meditate, but unlike TM, the technique is not to empty one's mind of all but the mantra, but instead to meditate on the Word of God. As we do this and as we allow our mind to be renewed to God's perspective on living, we become successful and prosperous in all aspects of life: relationships, business dealings, family, peace of mind. We become better people, we have peace, and we are full of Life!

"Blessed (happy, fortunate, prosperous, and enviable) is the man who walks and lives not in the counsel of the ungodly [following their advice, their plans and purposes], nor stands [submissive and inactive] in the path where sinners walk, nor sits down [to relax and rest] where the scornful [and the mockers] gather. But his delight and desire are in the law of the Lord, and on His law (the precepts, the instructions, the teachings of God) he habitually meditates (ponders and studies) by day and by night. And he shall be like a tree firmly planted [and tended] by the streams of water, ready to bring forth its fruit in its season; its leaf also shall not fade or wither; and everything he does shall prosper [and come to maturity]." Psalm 1:1-3 Amplified

"Do not let this Book of the Law depart from your mouth; meditate on it day and night, so that you may be careful to do everything written in it. Then you will be prosperous and successful." Joshua 1:8

Chapter 14

SUNWAYS, THE STORE

Sometime later, Frank the Federal Community Development guy came to see me again and asked if I wanted to run a handmade goods store. He had allocation of a storefront on Main Street, downtown Clarkston that was available for use during the Christmas holiday season. Frank saw me as an artisan that worked in metals and he knew of two other artisans who wanted to make money selling their handmade goods. Frank asked me to run the place and the Feds were to pay the utilities, clean up, and paint the place. I agreed. The store was a gift from God, but only for a season. One of the fellow vendors was a young woman high school dropout who handmade small leather items, purses, pouches, and such. The other was a slightly older guy who had just returned from 'Nam and couldn't find a job. He wanted to make sand candles.

Some time between the growing of the corn and the preparing to open the shop, the most significant event of my life took place: I accepted Jesus as my Savior and Lord. I was no longer an artisan making hashish pipes and Sterling silver roach clips, but instead I was a jewelry artisan, creating and crafting earrings, finger rings, and broaches. Previously I had crafted my own tools: blowtorches by alcohol, a ring mandrel from an old rifle barrel, and a kiln from heater coils from an old clothes dryer. I preferred to work mostly in silver although sometimes I worked in mixed media and occasionally in gold. Jewelry making was my therapy. It was my attempt to work out my growing anger, rage, and abusive behavior in what was considered to be a more socially acceptable way.

So everything seemed to be a go. I went down to City Hall and applied for a business license, and then I waited…and waited. Many days I sat in the shop wondering why the license was not being granted. Things were set up; goods were on display, but still no license. It never even occurred to me that my previous actions around town might have anything to do with the delay. When I talked to Chief Tilton, he said that they were waiting for a report from the FBI. "Yeah, and the moon is made out of blue cheese! You always ask for FBI reports on license applications? I'm sure!" I thought. Sometimes the devil will try to cause harm, but the Lord will turn it for good and that's certainly what happened in this case (as well as many other times in my life since)!

One day while still waiting patiently (as patiently as was possible for my temperament) for the license, I was sitting at my work table and a young boy came in and I promptly informed him that we weren't open yet. He appeared agitated and hurried, as he demanded he really needed to get something for a present—NOW. Taking pity on his situation, I acquiesced and told him to go ahead and pick something out. He glanced around and picked out a small leather pouch that Sarah, the High School Drop-out had made. He paid me for it and left. Later that same day, two young Clarkston police officers came in and asked if I was Tim Jones. I responded in the positive and then they proceeded to arrest me and ushered me down to the police station. I was arrested, booked and released on a charge of selling with out a Business License.

    Now this created a real catch 22. I went before a court judge about the charge of selling leather goods without a Business License and he concluded his judgment by stating that he could drop the charge if I obtained the necessary license. The conundrum came from the fact that the city of Clarkston was allegedly refusing to grant the license because there was an unresolved charge against me. It appeared there was no way out! I couldn't get the license because there was a charge against me and I couldn't get rid of the charge because I didn't have a license!

    Once again Frank came to my aide with his brilliant idea that we three artisans go before the City Council and relay to them how we needed to have this store to make some money to get back on our feet. It sounded like a solid plan and we had no other, so that's what we did! Frank arranged the meeting for us and we went with our best shot. When we arrived at the meeting, the Council Members sat at a long conference table with the mayor at the head and the other six members flanking the table, three abreast. To be sure, the scene was very imposing and the conference table might as well have been a wall, for the grim expressions on the Council Members' faces!

The first to give her appeal was the young woman, Sarah, who crafted the leather goods. She relayed how she had dropped out of high school and needed to sell these things to make a living for herself. The quality of her work was nice, but not outstanding and the real question in my mind was whether there was much market for her type of goods in Clarkston. My personal opinion was that she should get back into High School and graduate, but I kept my opinion to myself this time; after all, it was her life. Next the Candle man spoke and he tried to play the war veteran card. He elaborated on how he had just come back from 'Nam, couldn't find a job, had run out of money, and needed something to tide him over until he found some permanent employment. Today, the perception may be that the USA didn't support the troops when they came home from the Vietnam war and this may have been the case in much of America, however, the council was comprised of predominately older, fairly conservative upstanding members of this community who should be sympathetic to the plight of a war veteran if anyone would be. The expressions on the councilmen's faces and the comments that they were making did not bode well for our outcome, however.

One of the Council Members surmised he did not have enough information to vote for granting the license. I sat there for what seemed like forever; then it was my turn to speak. I postulated that the problem they were having in granting the license had to do with the head shop, "the Cheshire Cat." I recounted that I had placed some roach clips and hashish pipes on consignment there in the past, but had sold only a couple items total and that I had never participated in any of the drug trafficking that allegedly took place there. I went on to explain that I had since then been saved and delivered from drug usage by Jesus Christ. This information seemed to stir up the first glimmer of interest on their faces. They inquired as to where I was going to church and I gladly offered that I went to Faith Tabernacle on 10th and 10th in Lewiston, under Reverend Ray Tucker. They said they would have liked to hear from him. Quite honestly, it had never occurred to me to enlist his support. From that moment on, six of the Council Members' countenances changed; only the mayor's remained grim. The vote cast was six in favor of granting the license, and none against. I was glad that we didn't need the mayor's vote to break a tie!

Later, I found out that Frank published an article about the event, entitled, "Pulling the Teeth of the Alligator." It turns out the young boy who purchased the leather pouch had been sent by his dad, a merchant from a shop up the street, someone who had never come into the shop, had never spoken to me, had presumed a judgment about me, and meant me ill because of his preconceived ideas.

I am kind of a practical guy. I don't think too much about the finer nit-picky points of theology. I don't like to argue about how many angels can stand on the head of a pin, or whether God can make two mountains without a valley in between, or even, perhaps more relevant points, like pre, post or mid tribulation theory. I know that if I follow the Lord and His Word, all things will come out for my benefit and His Word will be realized in my life.

"Because the Sovereign Lord helps me, I will not be disgraced. Therefore have I set my face like flint, and I know I will not be put to shame. He who vindicates me is near. Who then will bring charges against me? Let us face each other! Who is my accuser? Let him confront me! It is the Sovereign Lord who helps me. Who is he that will condemn me? They will all wear out like a garment; the moths will eat them up." Isa 50:7,8,9

"We are assured and know that [God being a partner in their labor] all things work together and are [fitting into a plan] for good to and for those who love God and are called according to [His] design and purpose.....What then shall we say to [all] this? If God is for us, who [can be] against us? [Who can be our foe if God is on our side?] Romans 8:28, 31

"And I heard a loud voice saying in heaven, Now is come salvation, and strength, and the kingdom of our God, and the power of his Christ: for the accuser of our brethren is cast down, which accused them before our God day and night. And they overcame him by the blood of the Lamb, and by the word of their testimony;" Revelation 12:10-11 KJV

Chapter 15

The Job

When Frank set up the Store on Main Street in Clarkston, he said it would only be available through the Christmas Season. After Christmas he came and reminded me that the free rent was shortly coming to an end.

Although, I had become a Christian, my life was still in total disarray. My wife had left me because she needed to flee the abusive anger that had become an integral part of me; therefore I was living alone in a rental house on Second Street in Clarkston. Although the rent was only fifty dollars a month, I couldn't make it unless some of my jewelry sold. I had taken an order for a custom ring but it would not bring enough by itself. I had also made four pair of earrings from silver and Lapis stones; they were nice-- in fact some of my best work! I calculated that if I sold those earrings also, I could make my rent, but otherwise I was facing the possibility of being homeless. I had been homeless before by choice and it had been no big deal, but now I was a Christian and life was taking on a different perspective for me and I didn't want to be homeless.

I put the new earrings on the display table by the front door so they would be the first things a customer sees. I recalculated and figured that even if only a couple of these sold, I could still barely make my rent. It was now shortly after Christmas, and the after-Christmas store traffic was light, not that it ever had been very heavy even during the Holiday season. Nevertheless, I had high hopes as the earrings were especially fine, and I had priced them to sell quickly. A gaggle of customers came in the door: four high school-aged girls and the mother of one. What luck! The mother came in to purchase the custom ring her daughter had ordered. Great! Some of the rent money! And the girls were over at the table looking at the earrings! It was going to be a great day!... Or so I thought. The customers left and the shop returned to its normal quiet morgue feel, but I was bouncing from the floor to the ceiling I was so elated!! On the first bounce I looked at the table where the four pair of earrings were displayed. Three out to the four pair of earrings were gone! I went from bouncing to crash landing in a matter of seconds! What now!

I was now a Christian so it must be time to pray, I thought. I went in the back room and rattled the gates of heaven with my prayers! I began to pray in a prayer language and felt the Spirit of God tell me, "Go to Troy, there is a job waiting for you there." Uh huh, was it the Spirit of God or was it just the spirit of Tim Wishful Thinking? After all, my wife was living in Troy in a small rental house in an old part of town and I still wanted to

The Job

be married even if she didn't. At least we might be able to see each other. Neither of us had a car, so getting to Troy from Clarkston was not easy. The Big Grey Dog (Greyhound Bus) ran from Clarkston to Lewiston and another ran from Lewiston to Moscow but that still left about twelve miles of walking to get to Troy. Not only was reconciling with my wife tenuous, but the transportation hurdle was daunting, so did my mind really hear that I should go to Troy, or did I make it up?

Troy was a town of about 700 people total, maybe including some of the livestock. Although there was some new construction going on, most of the town had been built in the early twentieth century and I knew logically speaking, looking for employment in that small community was going to be tough. With all this in mind, I decided the only way to find out if there was a job for me was to actually go to Troy to find out. I put a sign on the door of the store, saying we were closed the rest of the day, and started walking. When I got to the highway I put my thumb out. Hitchhiking, even for a longhaired weirdo, was always easier in Idaho than it was in California. Anyway the less the traffic, the more likely I was to get a ride. Sometimes, a thousand cars passed me by on a busy freeway on-ramp, but on a lonely deserted road a ride was always offered within the first few cars. As I arrived in Troy I heard someone pounding nails in a house that was under construction. Although I felt that this was not the job for me, it occurred to me that it had been a long time since I had applied for a job and that a practice run might be in order. The worker I talked to said that the company was looking for laborers, but the application process took place at the office in Lewiston. I figure The Lord would lead me to Troy only to have to turn back to Lewiston to apply, so down the road I went. There were only a few places to look in Troy: a brick manufacturer, a mechanical/machine shop, and a cedar mill. The first place that I encountered on foot was Idaho Cedar Sales. I was fairly certain I didn't want to work in a mill as it was hard, dirty work--just what a city boy didn't want! However, I didn't want to miss what God had for me either, so I reluctantly broached the office door threshold and went in. The gal at the front desk affirmed they were looking for workers, but Leroy, the Plant Manager, wasn't in the office at the moment. Relief flooded me as I thought, "Great, I'm out of here, this is not what I wanted anyway!" As I turned to leave, she poked an application at me and asked me to fill it out. I filled out the application as fast as I could, hoping that Leroy didn't arrive before I finished and made my escape. I rationalized that no outfit hired for these types of jobs from an application, and I had no home phone for contacting, so if I departed before his arrival, I was free from the obligatory job inquiry and wouldn't have to take a job I did not want. As fast as I was filling out the application—and I can be really fast—I wasn't faster than God! Just as I finished the application and turned to give it to the secretary, the door opened and the Secretary exclaimed gleefully, "Oh, here is Leroy, now."

Leroy shook my hand, quickly looked at the application and then back at me and asked if I was good

The Job

with my hands. I responded that I had busted batteries in Lewiston at Pacific Hyde and Fur and with that nugget of information. I was hired. I was assigned to start work on the night crew as soon as they got the "Hog" fixed. I knew he couldn't be talking about the kind of hog that Great Grandpa Tim had raised and I couldn't imagine Leroy was saying he had to get his Harley repaired before I started work. The only other "hog" I knew of was a synthetic-Macrobiotic-psychedelic drug that caused a mess at the San Jose Pop festival.

I moved into my wife's house and waited, for what seemed like forever, while the hog was being repaired. This "hog" really had me baffled, and the wait was outlasting my patience, so I went down to the mill to check out the "Hog" one day. The Hog was a huge wood chipper that took the cedar scraps and made them into small chips for ground cover. It had a huge six-foot by six foot hopper fed by a conveyor belt that brought all the trimmings from the mill. A 500-horse power electric motor operated Hog's huge hammers and it was this motor that had fried just before I arrived on the scene. The local small electric shop downtown Troy, was rebuilding the motor and ordering parts, as there aren't too many 500 hp electric motors in the town of Troy, so it was a slow process, but eventually the Hog was up and running.

The work was physically hard and demanding, especially for someone that had become as lazy as I. Before the Lord removed the desire for cigarettes from my life, I had become so lazy that instead of reaching the ashtray on a table 5 or 6 feet away, I just flicked the ashes on the floor. However, it was evident my lazy days had abruptly come to a halt.

Leroy started me on the Little Splitter that first night. The Little Splitter was a misnomer because it was only little in relation to the Big Splitter. It consisted of a steel table about seven feet long by about one foot wide and half an inch thick. The Little Splitter had two ¾" thick, 7" wide steel blades that were connected by a chain like a bicycle chain, only long and bigger in link size. Only one blade was on top of the table at a time, while the other blade would be below the table and they were driven by a 25 horse power motor. The purpose of the Little Splitter was to split large six foot long, randomly wide and thick blocks of Cedar into fairly uniform thicknesses. These boards of still random widths were then pushed through a bank of carbide-tipped saws that made them into standard widths.

My job was to lift these six foot blocks that were as much as one foot thick, by eighteen inches wide and place it on the table. Then I was supposed to hold it with one hand; step on the motor pedal to activated the blades, and split a slab off. I had to hold the large block with one hand so the other hand could grab the split slab and toss it over to the next bin where the Pusher pushed the slabs through the saws. Is there any wonder that they prided themselves in being called Cedar Savages? So here I was recently saved, but still mostly peace love and granola-tea Tim trying to lift this hefty hunk of cedar. The first slab I lifted almost slipped out of my hand and for a split second I thought it was going to be a short career and a footless life! Then I felt a strange power come over my arm and my grip increased ten fold. My position on the Little Splitter only lasted a couple of days and then Leroy graduated me to the Big Splitter.

Now, the Big Splitter was a man eatin' killer machine. You might think that I'm just exaggerating but in the five years I worked there, two men lost thumbs and one had a heart attack from that machine. The machine was fed from the yard with Cedar logs that were sometimes six feet in diameter. They were old growth, the best kind for making pickets as they had straight grain with few or no knots and the clear wood made the Number One Grade pickets. These logs were cut into about seven foot lengths, then placed on a double chain that the Big Splitter Operator ran to bring the logs in position to the splitter. On the front end of his table was a six-foot blade that was inches thick and about a foot wide. This was attached to a hydraulic ram that was many feet long. The operator positioned the log to make the first cut and ran the blade into the log. If the log didn't split then he used the back plate to get even more power to split the log. The back plate had a ram that was slower but more powerful. The log was then split and the chain took one half away, and the second half was split again, and so on until the piece was small enough to handle--just barely! When the size was manageable, the block would be slung, by hand, onto another double chain, which cut off the ends to make a six-foot length, the length of the finished picket. If the piece was too knotty or not straight enough, it was thrown onto another double chain and sent to the post trimmer. I was supposed to run this machine on the night crew. Fortunately for me, the night shift was only six hours long, as it was more than I felt I could handle.

Just when I felt that I couldn't make it, help arrived in the form of a short, stout, amazingly strong man. This man was also a believer in Jesus Christ. In retrospect, I wonder if he was an angelic being in that he was just what I needed in all respects. At that time there were no Christians at the mill; in fact it was quite the opposite. One of the employees and relative to the boss had done time in the Idaho State Penitentiary and the company used beer and the enticement of a drinking party as a work performance incentive. The drunkenness was anticipated early in the week. When the Big Splitter Operator started splitting thick, clear cedar, someone would call out "Beer Wood". The rate of work picked up, and the saws and splitters hummed as the crew of four men and two women focused on the work. The yardmen sawed faster to make sure the Big Splitter chain was kept full of "Beer Wood". When this happened and if the wood held up, the crew would make more than two hundred bundles of pickets in a day. On any day the crew made two hundred or more bundles of pickets, the company bought a case of beer on Friday at the end of the day shift. Soon after I started on the night crew, the day crew made "Beer" four days in one week. Although the crew included the yardmen, and driller as well, four cases of beer was a good start for a crew of that size to get pretty drunk.

It was very refreshing to have a strong brother on the machine. He took the front end and I was on the back end, which was the easy one. I just lifted my end, while he lifted and threw his end onto the next chains. After some time I began to feel that I had gained significant amount of muscle strength. One night about the time I was beginning to see sufficient strength, my cohort and brother in the Lord told me he had another job, and it was his last night. I never saw him again. This brother was certainly God's provision for my need of the moment. He may have just been a man of flesh and blood, or he may have been an angelic being in the form of flesh, but I never saw or heard of him again in the seven years I worked in that small town and that close-knit group of workers. The Bible does talk of angelic beings coming in time of need and distress, and perhaps he was one for me, but whichever case, I felt very much like a way had been made for me.

The current philosophy of the era is that these events, as all the events that make up our lives, are just random occurrences in a random universe. But the events of my life, with the thoughts and experiences that precede them and the consistent, rational progression to a logical end make it impossible for me to believe the concept of a random universe. Sometimes we don't see the order in our world, like not being able to see the forest for the trees we keep seemingly randomly bumping into. I felt like at Idaho Cedar sales I caught my first glimpse where I could visually comprehend it, of God's plan to increase and bless me. I increased in strength, both physically and spiritually. Additionally, I was blessed financially with consistent, stable income for my family and me. There is nothing random about that.

"For I know the plans I have for you", declares the Lord, "plans to prosper you and not to harm you, plans to give you a hope and a future. Then you will call upon me and come and pray to me, and I will listen to you. You will seek me and find me when you seek me with all your heart." Jeremiah 29:11

"...for it is God Who is all the while effectually at work in you [energizing and creating in you the power and desire], both to will and to work for His good pleasure and satisfaction and delight." Phillipians 2:13

Chapter 16

SAN DIEGO

One year while living in Idaho we decided to go to Morris Cerullo's 10th Annual Deeper Life Conference, which was being held in San Diego, California. With three stair-step babies in tow, a car dependent on prayer as much as gas to get us there, and a Top Ramen budget, it was a mammoth effort for us to make the trip. But we wanted to delve feet first into our new Christian faith and we calculated we had enough money and food to get us there and back—barely! So we set off on an adventure, first stopping on the way at my Uncle Travis' house for an afternoon visit.

Uncle Travis had been a Christian for as long as I could remember. My dad, his brother, on the other hand was a very vocal agnostic who loved to play the "devil's advocate" to argue with him about religious things. Dad would not miss an opportunity at family holidays to strike up a not-so-friendly-tiff on religious nothingness.

However, Travis was a Gideon, whose aim is to get the Good News of the Gospel of Jesus Christ into everyone's hand in the form of a Gideon's New Testament Bible. This visit, Travis gave me some New Testaments. What on earth was I supposed to do with them? I hadn't a clue, but I took them, thanked him, and stashed them in the glove box of the van with the rest of life's little incidentals that don't seem to have a logical place but might come in handy someday.

THE EPILEPTIC

In our quest to the conference, we heard about a church that had some righteous bands playing radical non-traditional Christian music in their services so we decided to check it out since most churches at this time were stuck in the old died and fried hymns of the past. Now don't get me wrong, I could hardly be called zealous about being in church at this point. I was looking for a high. Reverend Ray Tucker the minister of the little church I attended in Lewiston, Idaho summed me up fairly well. After church one day, he said to me, "I know you only come for the buzz you get from the anointing of the Holy Ghost, but that's ok because while you're here, you get the Word of God also." It was true. The anointing of the Holy Spirit was like a natural high for me and was better than any drug I had ever smoked, toked, popped, or otherwise ingested. And the great thing about the Holy Spirit is that I felt better instead of worse the next day. A good time of worship in which I could feel the Presence of God gave me a certain measure of peace. Normal life for me had always included a high level of internal tension or agitation as long as I could remember. I found that the spiritual high gave me a short, but effective reprieve.

At the church, my wife and babies went to a room for mothers with small children where she could watch the service from closed circuit TV, so I was on my own. For some bizarre reason I started to get antsy about midway through the whole thing. I had this strange sensation that I needed to leave and go OUT. Out where? I didn't know, just out! I was enjoying the atmosphere and was reluctant to miss experiencing God. This sensation to leave seemed illogical; however I got up and exited from the auditorium. Once I did this, I thought to myself, "What on earth am I doing? I can't go anywhere anyway because I don't know where the closed circuit TV room is to get my wife". Once out, I was committed because there was no re-entry until the service was done once it had started. Out in front of the building I asked someone for directions to the closed circuit TV room.

Midway through his directions a passerby fell over with epileptic seizures only a few feet from where I was standing! His eyes were rolled back in his head and his body was held hostage by involuntary seizure, muscles tensed and contorted. My fellow on-looker cried, "Let's go get help!". I retorted, "Let's pray first." I bent over, touched him on the shoulder and prayed a simple prayer, something short and sweet. I didn't even know how to pray one of those fancy prayers! The seizures immediately stopped and he got up. He looked a little dazed, but otherwise appeared as if nothing had happened. No fanfare, just healing.

With musings of what had just transpired still in my head, I totally forgot about the closed circuit TV room and headed to my VW van. Once there, I found that my wife and kids had also come out to the car, completely unprompted and without explanation. How bizarre! It wasn't like we could communicate by cell phone in those days! What had we just encountered, but a moment orchestrated by the Divine.

"And these attesting signs will accompany those who believe: in My name they will drive out demons; they will speak in new languages; they will pick up serpents, and even if they drink anything deadly, it will not hurt them; they will lay their hands on the sick, and they will get well." Mark 16:17,18

THE HITCHHIKER

We took off in our Volkswagen bus and as we approached the city limits, we were still marveling at the synchronized timing of our departure. As we crested the Pacific Coast Highway junction, the sun was setting over the horizon, leaving the sky painted with intense lavenders, blues, and pinks, lending an almost mystical quality to the evening's events.

We spotted a hippie hitchhiking as we rounded the first bend and pulled over to pick him up. This hitchhiker was not more than 24 years old, and it was evident that he had been on the road for some time. His hair was long and snarly, constrained by a red bandanna crown across his temple, giving him a wild silhouette against the brilliant sky. His clothes were well worn and enveloped with an old army jacket, and his feet boasted a pair of dilapidated combat boots, scuffed and marred from countless miles of tread. But what was most intriguing about this man was his eyes. There was nothing worn, weary, or wild about them; his gaze was piercing and inquisitive as if he was looking for something and anticipated finding it at any turn.

As soon as the hitchhiker was comfy in the back seat of the van next to the children, a question popped out: "Do you know Jesus Christ?" I suppressed an urge to turn my head to see who might have said these words, because I knew that, in truth, they had come out of my own mouth. He replied that he had heard of Him. I responded that I had heard of Richard Nixon, but it didn't mean I really knew him. Hearing of Jesus and knowing Him are very different things, I countered.

This vagabond then relayed to us how he had gone on a journey to India, searching for a guru—someone who could illuminate God to him. He wanted to find meaning for his life. Upon his return to the States he visited old friends in the Bay area that were living in a hippie Christian commune and these were the friends that had spoken to him about Jesus. But he reasoned he wasn't ready to accept Him into his life because he needed to check out a few more things. I remembered the New Testaments I had stashed in the glove box. Now I understood why Uncle Travis felt prompted to give me those New Testaments! I gave him one so that he could read the Good News for himself and I suggested that he start with the Gospel of John. With as much said, our brief encounter was over. We dropped him off at the junction and our paths diverged.

I am still amazed at how far the Father will go, and how many different people He will use to bring one person into His kingdom. I am confident that this hitchhiker's search for meaning ended when He met Jesus through reading that little New Testament and I will see him again in heaven!

"So neither he who plants is anything nor he who waters, but only God Who makes it grow and become greater" I Cor 3:7

THE AFRICAN PRINCESS

We continued our trek down to San Diego. The conference was held in one of San Diego's hotels downtown in the conference auditorium, which had a stage, theater chair seating, and tiers of balcony seating as well. There were speakers during the day, healing services at night, and lunches served in an adjacent banquet room. One day after the lunch, I felt prompted out of the blue to get out of my chair and take a walk across the sky bridge from the banquet room toward the lobby of the hotel. On the sky bridge, a tall, stately woman approached me. It was clear from her attire that she was from an African nation. She wore a bright multi-colored traditional tribal dress and her head was crowned with a turban that was equally ornate and colorful. I surmised from her extraordinary regal bearing that she was someone of high position and purpose. Upon seeing me, this woman inquired as to where she might find Morris Cerrello. It seemed like an oxymoron moment. Here was this stately woman, so very out of context to her station and nation walking the sky bridge of this hotel and here was I, a long-haired hippie in jeans without a clue as to why I felt so compelled to walk the sky bridge. I felt like the donkey God used to talk to Balaam in the Bible. I didn't know what I was doing or why, but I was encountering this regal woman. I directed her to where he was seated in the banquet hall and instead of resuming my quest on the sky bridge; I sat back down in my chair, inwardly sensing that my quest was accomplished when I directed this elegant lady to her destination.

At the opening of the afternoon session the woman's identity and purpose were disclosed. She was introduced as an African tribal princess of a great nation and her purpose was to act as diplomatic emissary for her nation toward Morris Cerullo. She presented him with brightly colored tribal garb for his humanitarian efforts, his huge monetary support of a school and his significant advancement in training nationals to educate their own people in the ways of Christ.

To some, this event may seem rather insignificant. It didn't involve a healing or miracle, but it holds a very significant nugget of truth. God uses what and who are available for His purposes. He can use a donkey to stop a man from reckless living; he can use a hippie to escort a princess. He orders the footsteps of any willing to heed

His promptings. Additionally, He honors those that are His emissaries by guiding them and providing direction through others and making a way for them in unfamiliar surroundings.

Story of the Donkey   Numbers 22:20-31

"Trust in the Lord with all your heart and lean not on your own understanding; acknowledge him in all yours ways and he shall direct your paths" Proverbs 3: 5,6

THE TEENAGERS

At one of the subsequent meetings, Morris Cerrello promised a healing service the following night and asked the hundreds of attendees to fast a meal for it. The scripture: *"and whosoever shall compel thee to go a mile, go with him twain" (Matt 5:41 KJV)*, popped into my head. With this verse in mind, I decided to fast two meals instead of one. Morris Cerullo then asked for a show of hands of those who committed to this fast. Another verse popped into my head: *"Then, when you fast, don't look like those miserable play-actors! For they deliberately disfigure their faces so that people may see that they are fasting. Believe me, they have had all their reward. No, when you fast, anoint your head and wash your face so that nobody knows that you are fasting—let it be a secret between you and your Father. And your Father who knows all secrets will reward you." (Matthew 6:16-18, Phillips Translation)*

Although most of the attendees raised their hands in agreement, I determined to fast, but keep it to myself.

Later that evening and all the next day as I walked around the hotel complex, I observed several groups of teenagers in the process of setting up for music performances. Their actions were not illegal or inappropriate, but as I watched them, I sensed a state of confusion and chaos that enveloped them. What I saw and perceived in the spirit prompted me to pray specifically for deliverance for teenagers.

At the promised healing service the following evening Morris Cerrello came out and asked how many people wanted to do God's will. Although he had promised a healing service, he felt very strongly that he needed to do the Father's will and that was to make an appeal to the teenagers in the crowd. It was evident that he struggled with this because he had already given his word for a healing service and there were people who needed healing and were expecting it. But he verbalized to the crowd that what the Lord had told him to do, was more important for the moment. He gave a short appeal to the teenagers, only a few minutes. He asked them to come to the base of the stage and stand with him if they wanted deliverance. Even before he could get the appeal spoken, teenagers seemed to be materializing from nowhere, coming out of seats, and coming from the balcony! The base of the stage was a wall-to-wall teenager and they were throwing their cigarettes, drugs and alcohol onto the stage in an act of faith to be delivered!

There was an incredible response to Morris

Cerullo's appeal and it was impressive to watch. I felt like I was in a dream as I watched the teenagers sobbing, kneeling, and lifting their hands in adoration. I had seen the Lord's heart earlier that day as I observed those teenagers and sensed their need for Him. Here was the tangible answer to that need!

"For My thoughts are not your thoughts, neither are your ways My ways, declares the Lord. As the heavens are higher than the earth, so are My ways higher than your ways and My thoughts than your thoughts.....So shall My word be that goes forth out of My mouth: it shall not return to Me void [without producing any effect, useless], but it shall accomplish that which I please and purpose, and it shall prosper in the thing for which I sent it." Isaiah 55:8,9,11

CANCER

There were healing services on other evenings, with always a long line of testimonials of what the Lord had done. The one that impressed me most was a testimony that never made it to the stage. After for prayer for healing on night, an usher approached the man sitting in the row in front of me. The usher asked, "Did God do something for you? The man replied, "Yes."
Usher: "What did God do?"
Man: "He healed me."
Usher: "What did He heal you of?"
Man: "Cancer"
Usher: "Where did He heal you?"
Man: "Here, in my body."

SAN DIEGO

Usher: "How do you know?"
Man: "There was a lump right here, but now it is gone." (The man was indicating his abdominal area.)
The usher and the man left to go discuss it with someone else. "How odd!" I thought. I never saw this man get on the stage to tell his story about being healed. If the testimonials were faked, would they fake one man for those few in the immediate area?" I asked myself. For me, this man's testimony gave tangible credence to the fact that Jesus really does heal even still. Not because of the hoopla of preachers on a stage or for vainglory, but because He loves people and has compassion on us all.

"When He (Jesus) went ashore and saw a great throng of people, He had compassion for them and cured their sick." Matthew 14:14

"A man with leprosy came to him and begged him on his knees, "If you are willing, you can make me clean." Filled with compassion, Jesus reached out his hand and touched the man. "I am willing", he said. "Be clean!" Immediately the leprosy left him and he was cured." Mark 1:40-42

The conference came to a close and we trundled our family home in our VW bus. We arrived home with the gas gage on "E", two very bald tires that had amazingly stayed intact for us, and less then $1.00 in our pockets, but we also arrived with a mountain of memories and experiences, as much as our hearts could contain for the moment.

For this young follower of Jesus, the lessons learned were profound. They were not lessons delineated by the 12-step program or the 5-step program, or any other program. They could not possibly have been orchestrated by some human, no, they were written by the hand of the One Who knows me best and loves me most. I was just beginning to see how much!

"For I know the plans I have for you", declares the Lord, "plans to prosper you and not to harm you, plans to give you a hope and a future".
Jeremiah 29:11

Chapter 17

THE PREACHER WITH FIRE IN HIS EYE

    I have heard it said by some Idahoans that Idaho is God's country. It is true that Idaho is a beautiful state and I have fond memories of living on the high plains and hiking up the Selway River and in the Palouse and whitewater rafting down the Salmon River. These spots are all near and dear to my heart, but the thing that Idaho has had for the last many decades that I am most appreciative of is a preacher with fire in his eye.

    Reverend Tucker, as he is now known, is overseer of numerous churches in Idaho and travels often to Africa to mentor many national church pastors; he also oversees a gospel TV station that reaches Northern Idaho; but back in my hippie days in the '70's he was known as Brother Tucker and was pastor of a small, but growing, assembly of believers in Lewiston, Idaho. Brother Tucker, a piano refinisher, by trade, was called by God to be a preacher, so he closed the doors of his shop and obeyed the call. He was not a seminary graduate; not even a highly educated man. But he took the gifting God gave him, took the promises of the Bible at face value, and believed God for the rest. As a result, God has done some amazing things through this man.

I met Brother Tucker and, therefore, Faith Tabernacle Church while living in Clarkston, (just across the river from Lewiston) Idaho soon after I accepted Jesus into my life. Within the year, however, I took a job at a cedar mill in Troy. My family and I lived in Troy and we commuted the hour's drive one way to Faith Tabernacle several times a week.

One of the amazing things about Brother Tucker was his discernment in the Holy Spirit. One day when I was still fairly new to this Jesus stuff, Brother Tucker came up to me and revealed that he knew the secrets of my heart. He said that I was coming to church for the high that I got from there-- that I would feel the anointing of the Holy Ghost during worship. It was so true! I attended Sunday morning, Sunday evening, and Tuesday evening services just for the feeling I got from the worship. I didn't go to the Thursday Bible study because there was no worship and therefore no buzz for me. Then he went on to say that it was ok, because I was getting the Word at the same time. I so loved the anointing! I have never before or since felt the intensity of the Holy Spirit's Presence as I did in Faith Tabernacle, Lewiston, Idaho.

In Isa 55:11 it says: "So shall my word be that goes forth out of my mouth: it shall not return to me void [without producing any effect, useless], but it shall accomplish that which I please and purpose, and it shall prosper in the thing for which I sent it." (Amp)

THE PIMP AND THE PROSTITUTE

Brother Tucker was known in the Palouse for having a healing ministry. I have no doubt that if I researched and found those who had received a healing of some kind during one of Brother Tucker's meetings, the numbers would be astounding. One story that I heard sticks with me to this day. One day while helping the church renovate a building to launch a ministry halfway house for recovering addicts, I listened to the story of an ex-pimp named Victor. While we worked side by side, pulling out nails, removing old lumber, and then replacing it with new, we had ample hours of time to talk.

Victor had been a pimp starting in San Jose, then running to Seattle, Washington and had pimped for a prostitute named Cheryl. Victor was a tall, thin, black guy. He seemed friendly enough and was rather talkative. Cheryl, a blonde, blue-eyed slender woman, had a sister that had accepted the Lord some time before. She and her husband and family attended Faith Tabernacle on Tenth and Tenth St, in Lewiston. Cheryl and Victor came to Lewiston to visit Cheryl's sister. While they were visiting, Cheryl's sister invited them to church and they agreed to go. But, Victor was so strung out that he felt he had to hit up with some smack before going. So he went into the bathroom and did some heroin and then they went off to church with Victor flying high. At the end of the service when Brother Tucker invited people to come forward to receive salvation, who of all people wanted to go forward? Victor. He told Brother Tucker he wanted to be saved, but that he had been on a two and a half year run of heroin. Brother Tucker said no problem. He explained that first they would pray for Salvation, then deliverance. They prayed together for Salvation. Then Brother Tucker prayed that God, through the Name of Jesus, would set Victor free from heroin addiction.

As we continued to hammer and replace boards, Victor related to me how he had left the church service that night and went back to Sue's sister's house and sat around as though in a daze for three days. He didn't go through any symptoms of withdrawal. No sweating, stomach cramps, nausea, nothing! This was so awesome!

When Cheryl saw how changed Victor was and how he was able to conquer drugs without the demon withdrawal, she wanted it too. So the next service, she went forward and asked for salvation and deliverance. She, too, was saved and delivered. No withdrawal symptoms, only a lifting of the huge burden in her heart that had been there for so long!

God is real and His deliverance is real! What we do with God's gifts is critical. Apparently, Victor and Cheryl made different choices. Many years after Victor told me of what God had done for Cheryl and him, I went back to the church in Lewiston. Due to continued growth, it had changed locations. The old location was still used, for the gospel TV station, but not regular services. We went to church in the new location and after the service; Reverend Tucker invited us to lunch. Over lunch I asked him if he knew anything about Victor and Cheryl and how they were doing 20+ years later. The news was bittersweet. The church had started a half way house as planned, but it didn't attract enough reformed addicts to sustain operation and justify its existence, so it was closed. Victor back to Seattle but instead of falling back into the old life he had known there before, he became involved in a Teen Challenge program. Teen Challenge is a program where recovering addicts live for a pre-specified amount of time such as a year. They spend lots of time reading scripture and renewing their minds with Godly principles and incorporating a gradual changing of their lifestyle. Then the drugs are not needed any more. The Teen Challenge Program was, and still is, THE MOST EFECTIVE Program for drug rehabilitation that has been studied in the USA. Its success rate is about ten times as good as that of government funded programs. It worked for Victor. He stayed off drugs and shared the amazing work of Jesus in his life with others in the gym or wherever he was, and last I have heard he is preaching the Gospel in California.

    The last Reverend Tucker had heard of him, he was preaching the Gospel. Although Cheryl started in the Faith Tabernacle Half way house she did not stay in a program. She went back to the street and drugs. She was subsequently was found murdered and dismembered. A form of murder that was believed to have been used by the mob in that area, at that time as a form of punishment for those that broke the mobs rules of drug trade.

    This particular incident demonstrates some really

important points. The first is embodied in the scripture, *" Therefore God also has highly exalted Him and given Him the name which is above every name, that at the name of Jesus every knee should bow, of those in heaven, and of those on earth, and of those under the earth"*
Phil 2:9-10 (NKJV).
The name of Jesus is above every name that is named. It doesn't matter what name is called out, alcohol, methadrine, or heroin. The name of Jesus is more powerful. Do we have the faith? Brother Tucker did those nights that the heroin was cast out. Sometimes we have so little faith that we don't stand on, or declare God's Word when faced with strong enemies, such as alcohol and heroin. But, if we have faith and declare God's Word, he is faithful. His Word declares, *"For as the rain comes down, and the snow from heaven, And do not return there, But water the earth, And make it bring forth and bud, That it may give seed to the sower And bread to the eater, So shall My word be that goes forth from My mouth; It shall not return to Me void, But it shall accomplish what I please, And it shall prosper in the thing for which I sent it. "For you shall go out with joy, And be led out with peace; The mountains and the hills Shall break forth into singing before you, And all the trees of the field shall clap their hands. Instead of the thorn shall come up the cypress tree, And instead of the brier shall come up the myrtle tree; Isaiah 55:10-13 (NKJV)*

This scripture clearly points out how God will take out the briers and thorns in our lives and replace them with beautiful things like Cyprus and Myrtle trees. When the biers of addictions and ungodly habits have been removed, and the new trees of Life have been planted, it is imperative that the new trees receive sufficient water for good growth. When the Pimp chose to get into a Teen challenge program, he was assured of getting 'watered'. This program has intensive times of Bible study and worship. For some reason the Prostitute choose not to get the watering of the Word that is so necessary for the renewing of the mind and the growth that produces a healthy tree or lifestyle.

"When a defiling evil spirit is expelled from someone, it drifts along through the desert looking for an oasis, some unsuspecting soul it can bedevil. When it doesn't find anyone, it says, 'I'll go back to my old haunt.' On return it finds the person spotlessly clean, but vacant. It then runs out and rounds up seven other spirits more evil than itself and they all move in, whooping it up. That person ends up far worse off than if he'd never gotten cleaned up in the first place. "That's what this generation is like: You may think you have cleaned out the junk from your lives and gotten ready for God, but you weren't hospitable to my kingdom message, and now all the devils are moving back in." Matt 12:43-45 (MSG)

If we are constantly renewing our mind, then we don't give the enemy any chance to come back to the swept house, our life. Sometimes I've heard Christians say, "God understands, I can --, insert, whatever the current issue is." Yes, God does understand. He understands that he does not ask us to do anything that he has not enabled us to do either.

"For no temptation (no trial regarded as enticing to sin), [no matter how it comes or where it leads] has overtaken you and laid hold on you that is not common to man [that is, no temptation or trial has come to you that is beyond human resistance and that is

not adjusted and adapted and belonging to human experience, and such as man can bear]. But God is faithful [to His Word and to His compassionate nature], and he [can be trusted] not to let you be tempted and tried and assayed beyond your ability and strength of resistance and power to endure, but with the temptation He will [always] also provide the way out (the means of escape to a landing place), that you may be capable and strong and powerful to bear up under it patiently. Therefore, my dearly beloved, shun (keep clear away from, avoid by flight if need be) any sort of idolatry (of loving or venerating anything more than God)." I Corinthians 10:13,14

JOHN AND THE OCCULT

Brother Tucker was a preacher that not only discerned truth accurately, but he delivered it with authority and conviction of purpose. I had made an acquaintance named John while living in Troy. John and I were both about the same age and being in a small community, we saw each other often. Over time, John told me about some of his experiences. He was a math teacher at the local High School and prior to my knowing him had been a "missionary" to Turkey in a program where he gained admittance to the country, worked, and made contacts for potential evangelism opportunities through his occupation as a math teacher. The only thing is that he never really shared the good news of Jesus Christ with anyone. He said that the Muslim Turks fired a cannon several times a day to mark out the Muslim prayer times, and when they did, they loaded rocks into the cannons and shot them at the Christian compound where John taught. Did this have anything to do with his decisions later in life? Who knows? But some time after returning to the States he began dabbling with Ouija boards, backward writing, and other practices associated with the occult. On occasion we talked about church. I had invited him occasionally and he would always respond with a polite, but firm decline.

Much to my surprise, one Sunday late afternoon, just before my family and I were leaving for the evening service, John called and asked to go to church with us. I said sure and stopped by his place to pick him up. Although he was only a few minutes off the road, we were late to church and by the time we got there the worship portion had already started so we quietly seated ourselves toward the back.

The worship portion of the service proceeded as usual but Brother Tucker ended it earlier than normal. He came to the podium and started to speak as though to a particular individual. He pointed out that this individual thought that he was a Christian and that he had even been sent abroad as a missionary, but that he had never shared the gospel with anyone. Although Brother Tucker had never met John and I had never mentioned nor spoken about John, John's spiritual life was painted in bright vivid colors by the Holy Ghost through the Message of Brother Tucker. The Ouija board, backward writings and other occult practices that John had used and had related to me, were all lined out. Brother Tucker related exactly the picture of my friend and told him he needed to get right with God. There was authority in his voice and it really looked like he had a red flame in one of his eyes.

Did John soften his heart? Not from his body language! His countenance was grim and he sat there like a stone with his arms folded across his chest. Everything about his demeanor said, "I defy you!" The service did not proceed as normal. No announcements were given, no offering taken; only worship and the manifestation of the Holy Ghost for one lost soul. Eventually Brother Tucker gave an invitation for those who wanted to be saved to come to the front by the podium. John sat there, his eyes and body reflecting his stony heart.

One young man came up to the front seeking salvation and Brother Tucker said that he was glad that the man came forward but that this was not the one that was being spoken to. Once again he called for the one to whom God was speaking to come forward. John never to my knowledge accepted the Lord's invitation. But what I saw that day was grace and mercy extended to this man. And I saw the passion in Brother Tucker's eyes, a reflection of the passion of the Almighty God for each of us. I heard the authority with which he delivered the message from The Father to John. I will never forget the preacher with the fire in his eye!

I no longer live in Idaho, but instead, now live in a state reported as being one of the most un-churched states in the Union. My perspective is that we just need to reclaim it as God's Country along with Idaho and all the rest! Idaho might be considered by some to be God's country, but in my estimation, it is all God's country. We need to see more men of passion that have a fire in their eye who will discern accurately and speak with authority, men who will stand up for what is right for all of God's country and see the amazing things that God desires to do on this earth and in peoples' lives.

"With great power the apostles continued to testify to the resurrection of the Lord Jesus, and much grace was upon them all." Acts 4:33

Chapter 18

THE SAINT MARIES FISHING TRIP

Some men are born to fish. There is something about fishing that draws them back to the body of water, no matter how big or small for that allurement of a bite or nibble or, oh, if they could be so lucky-- as the biggest fish, best fight on the line, longest play on the real! This is unquestionably not me. I have vivid memories of my father on his fishing boat drinking double martini's and the boat seemed to always need some repair for it to function right. The fish were elusive; the talk was negative, and my father drunk. These were not happy memories!

But one day my friend Larry, a CPA student at the University of Idaho and a fellow Christian asked me if I wanted to go fishing on the Saint Maries River in upstate Idaho. The thought of spending some time with a Bother and enjoy the beautiful outdoors sounded appealing to this novice Christian, so I agreed to go. The trip included some fishing, but hey, I could put up with a downside for all the other benefits. Another guy, whom I nicknamed Mountain Goat, for reasons soon revealed to us all, joined us.

So I dug my long-forgotten fishing gear out of the bottom of the closet and off we went. The day was a typical beautiful Idaho fall day. The air was crisp, but the sun radiated warmth. Mountain Goat was aptly nicknamed. He knew a fishing hole that he was sure was virtually un-fished. He took charge of the expedition, and with a wave of his arm and a "Follow me!" he led us directly into the river! I watched him start fording through the rushing water and thought, "well, if the short guy can do it, I guess I can too". At this time, I was a burly 6'4" Cedar Savage from working at the Cedar mill. I tossed logs into the saw mill like they were toothpicks all day long. Logs had honed my muscles into strength and I was confident of my abilities. Huh! Certainly I could keep up with anything he might come up with!

Larry and I delved into the rushing water. At the point where we forded, the river was about 150 ft wide, but only up to my waist deep. The chilled water felt refreshing after hiking in the sun, but the current was swift, tugging and pulling at my legs, and my footing was slick and unsure. It took all of my concentration to keep my footing and make it across. I marveled at how the 2 shorties were succeeding!

With only a short rest on the far bank of the river, Mountain Goat was off again. He said that there was a way over the top of the next large hill, but that there was a shortcut trail. I can now say that it should have been called a shortcut 'trial' instead of a 'trail'. Because that's exactly what it was! Off he went, straight up this narrow little goat trail. In a matter of a few huffs and puffs we were perched 100-plus feet above the now foaming whitewater ribbon of river with nothing but sheer vertical rock between it and us! The view was spectacular! Our little goat trail began narrowing dramatically. Now we cautiously advanced single file. On our right was a sheer wall of rock; on our left were air and a plummet to rocks and white foamy death. Our breathtaking view alarmingly now took on a more somber perspective. It took our breath away as our visual reminder of how frail life is, how precarious our position was, and how critical a slip in our toehold would be! It was at this very juncture that Larry abruptly froze. Fear was radiating from his eyes as clear as a neon signpost. Mountain Goat was now completely out of sight, oblivious to any hindrance of his reluctant followers whatsoever. At this point I was acutely aware of my abhorrence and therefore avoidance of heights! No fishing trip is worth this! But this day I found myself in a uniquely undesirable predicament having to decide to increase the height and press forward or retrace my unsteady steps. At this moment a blanket of terror enveloped me and arrested me body, soul and mind! It wasn't a rational fear, if fear can ever be called rational, but instead it was a heart-seizing terror that inhibited me from taking a step forward, or taking a step backward. It was like it tyrannized my very soul. I would have sworn I heard an audible voice that said, "There is no way out! You might as well jump!"

    Now, from where I was standing, I could see Larry's face clearly and his lips weren't moving! This moment cleared up any lingering doubt I might have had about the existence of the Devil and his desire for our ill. The devil comes to destroy, to seek out whom he can devour. That day Larry and I could have easily been his lunch! However, I knew I had a resource for overcoming this supernatural spirit of fear. I said to Larry, "Let's pray!" He nodded ascent, I began to pray and then went into a prayer language that some call 'tongues' In a matter of moments the fear fell off me like someone had come along with a pair of scissors and cut off the mummy bandages of fear entwined around me. I looked at Larry and could tell even without verbal affirmation that the same release had happened for him as well. We decided following a mountain goat should be left to the goats. We retraced our steps with uncanny surety in our every step. We reached the junction with the woods trail, trekked through the woods, and met Mountain Goat at the stream. The fish were bountiful, as promised and it did not take us long to fill our limit. It is easy to see why it was such a gem of a fishing spot with the magnitude of challenge to get there. One had to be dedicated to fishing to make the trip!

    My experience up on the crags above what momentarily looked like our whitewater grave, gave me cause to think. There was something very real, solid, about what little I had learned of the Christian faith thus far. I knew what had happened up there was for real and it made an indelible impact on me. Fishing was ok, but if I'm going to be dedicated to something, and passionate about anything, Jesus is a far better bet for my money!

The Saint Maries Fishing Trip

"There is no fear in love—dread does not exist; but full-grown (complete, perfect) love turns fear out of doors and expels every trace of terror!…" 1 John 4:18 Amp

"For God did not give us a spirit of timidity—of cowardice, of craven and cringing and fawning fear—but He has given us a spirit of power and of love and of calm and well-balanced mind and discipline and self-control." II Timothy 1:7

Chapter 19

The U of I

After working in the mill for many years, I looked for a way to escape. I remember one of the older guys--he must have been about forty--having a heart attack while working on the Big Splitter and it occurred to me that it was high time to get out of Idaho Cedar Sales and on to something less risky for life and limb. I went to the nearby University of Idaho and applied for entrance, however, to my chagrin, I was denied! The reason I was given for the denial was I didn't have a cumulative 2.0 G.P.A. from my previously attended colleges and universities. However, after flunking out of Long Beach State College (now California State University at Long Beach), with a whopping .9 GPA, I had attended various Junior Colleges until I had a 2.0 G.P.A....at least according to my calculations! Therefore, not wanting to take "NO" for an answer, I scheduled an appointment with the Dean of Admissions to defend my case, whereby pointing out how they had incorrectly calculated the GPA. He granted me admission based on my argument! (or was it divine intervention?)

Next I applied for financial aid and after the usual wait the Financial Aid Office told me they had good news and bad news for me. I qualified for $14,000 a year of financial aid; that was the good news. The bad news, or so they thought, was that they could only fund me at $11,000 a year due to funding shortages. I laughed out loud! Working hard and risking my body and limbs had only yielded me a little over $7,000 a year, so in essence, I was being given a pay raise to go to school! It was a funny twist of events, but I was in!

That summer of 1976 I drove to Moscow, eleven miles away from Troy, and walked around the campus deliberating on a course of study to pursue. I seriously considered law as I always liked to debate and argue--and win, of course. I entertained Engineering, as I knew I had aptitude for it and I would be good at it. Education had a higher purpose and that sounded noble. But it seemed there were no professors or advisors to discuss what I needed, except Doctor Ray Paloutzian of the Psychology Department. Dr. Paloutzian, as it turns out, was a Social Psychologist—and a Christian! To me this was a revolutionary concept. In my thinking, the two were mutually exclusive.

We talked for quite a while and we swapped stories of how we had become believers and followers of Jesus Christ. He told me of his heritage and how his family had survived the ethnic cleansing of Christian Armenians by the Turks at the start of the Twentieth Century. The Turks murdered over a million Armenian Christians in that slaughter; it is a black smudge on World History that most people are not even aware of today. The way Ray recounted the story is that God spoke to Ray's grandfather, warned him of the coming genocide, and told him to get himself and his family out of Armenia, so they left and came to America.

At this point in my life, I held the opinion that psychology was not a good field of study for a Christian. Most psychologists didn't believe in the reality of God speaking to man; hearing voices was easily explained away as a symptom of Schizophrenia. However hypnosis and other psychological practices seemed acceptable, even if they were opposed to Biblical principle. The biggest problem I observed with psychology was it's relatively powerless impact. Essentially psychology doesn't have the power to change people; therefore psychologists attempt to rationalize as to why everything from homosexuality to killing unborn babies must be ok. But, as I left Ray's office, and was walking back to my car I realized that I had stayed a lot longer than I had intended. Time had virtually evaporated as I listened enthralled to this interesting man. And as I walked the lower part of the campus, my whole body started to tingle as though I had just walked into a large and strong electrostatic field. It reminded me strikingly of an electrostatic field that had been produced by a Vander Graff generator. At that same moment, although I did not hear an audible voice,

I undeniably felt that God said to me, "That is where I want you to go."

This revelation was of great difficulty for me since I had already tried psychology through numerous psychologists and counselors to address my problems and found it pitifully wanting. I had been acutely aware of their lack of genuine caring for my situation but their genuine motivation for remuneration. I did not understand why God would have me go into this field, however when registration came around I declared my major as Psychology in spite of not knowing what benefit might be obtained or what the outcome would be.

Dr. Ray Paloutzian taught many interesting things relating to psychology and religion and his teaching has a good deal of influence in my thinking even today. In one of his classes he talked about the relationship between psychology and the Bible. There are three opposing philosophies concerning the Bible and Psychology among the psychological disciplines. Some psychologists think psychology is the final authority over the Bible; some think they are on equal footing; and others believe the Bible is the final authority over psychology. To Dr. Paloutzian and me, the Bible is the truth and final authority in man's relationship to God, and is above that of psychology. Psychology is always changing because it is comprised of men's thoughts; however, human concepts and philosophies change with the wind. But Jesus is the Rock; he is the same today, yesterday and forever.

As I delved into my studies and into the data in psychological experiments and statistics, the fundamental instability and weakness of psychology as a means to permanently cause positive impact on the human condition became even more glaringly apparent. One such study looked at the long-term effects of therapies and determined that although therapies might show results in patients initially, their effectiveness dwindled to nothing over the course of time. Other studies showed that for a subject (person) with mild neurosis, talking to a friend was as effective as paying a therapist. One that particularly intrigued me was a study that deduced that the first visit to a therapist, regardless of the therapy, was significantly more effective than later visits. This is really interesting since the first visit is often used by the therapist for the purpose of gathering general client information and establishing what the client's problem is.

I found myself asking a very elemental question as I studied: What is the common issue in all these things? To me the common underlying issue that is there is: faith. But wait, these aren't necessarily "people of faith", how can they have faith? God has placed in every man some faith, not just Christians. This faith is placed in any number of different things: the occult, various forms of witchcraft, archaeological science, personal strength and abilities, urban legends, medical science, superstition, education, titles of prestige, money, prescriptions, molecular science and research, drugs, alcohol, psychology. It's a matter of what we do with our faith that is the issue. Will the thing we place our faith in ultimately bring us the healing, resolution of problems, happiness, long-term peace of mind that we all essentially seek? Jesus' claim in the Bible is that He will in truth bring us all of these things when we place our faith in Him and the many promises of the Bible. To place our faith in Him does not necessarily negate the ability of most of these things listed above to assist us, but when Jesus is allowed to be Lord in our lives, He brings wisdom and order to our situations and can facilitate the use of the resources we have to accomplish a lasting change in our life and in our spirit. Jesus Christ's claims need to be seriously considered.

"But to think soberly, according as God hath dealt to every man the measure of faith." Rom 12:3 KJV

"So then faith cometh by hearing, and hearing by the word of God. " Romans 10:17 KJV

"Jesus answered, "I am the way and the truth and the life. No one comes to the Father except through me." John 14:6

GLOSSOLALIA

When I deliberated on a research topic for my thesis, I thought about the people in the Old Time Gospel church. These people were really big on praying in other tongues, and told stories of true events that supported their belief in the practice. Often they talked about how good they felt after "praying through to the Holy Ghost." One church member, Sister Cantola, related a graphic story to me about praying in tongues, or 'praying in the Holy Ghost': Sister Cantola awakened one night with a "heavy burden" for her grandson who was stationed with the U.S. forces in Vietnam, so she "prayed in the spirit" until the burden was removed. To extract this story from Pentecostal jargon, it might be said that she awoke and was excessively worried about her grandson and therefore she prayed in a prayer language to God until the worry was completely gone and then went back to bed. Some days after this prayer session, she received a letter from her grandson in which he relayed how at the very time Sister Cantola was praying for him, he had been standing next to an ammunition storage shed and God spoke to him and told him to run and get out of there. He did so and the moment he was out of range, a Viet Cong mortar shell hit the shed, causing a huge ammunition explosion, but his life was spared from what would have been certain death. This young soldier's letter expounded by saying that the voice of God he had heard that night sounded just like his grandmother's and as a result of this life-defining moment, he had dedicated his life to God, and intended to preach the Gospel!

These church members' descriptions of the Holy Ghost and benefits of praying in the Holy Ghost coincided with my encountering a "Popular Science" article enumerating how the Transcendental Meditation proponents measured brainwave activity of people that practiced TM. They reported that Transcendental Meditation produced an increased amount of Alpha Wave activity, thereby giving the subjects an increased buzz, or feeling of good and well-being. From my point of view, this sounded very much like the same report I was hearing from the Pentecostals and I was immensely intrigued!

    Let me interject at this point, that my dad and step mom taught me that all religions were basically the same. Even though Eugenia, my stepmother, was Jewish, she sent her daughters to the church across the street, which happened to be Methodist. They were all the same to her, so it didn't matter. I took what my father and stepmother said as fact, so early on, I too thought all religions were essentially the same. With this as my premise, I postulated praying in tongues would produce more alpha wave activity just like Transcendental Meditation did. My curiosity was piqued and I wanted to test it to see if my theory was correct! As it turns out, God was going to give me the chance!

    My core belief, at that time, that all religions were the same would soon be shattered. If all religions were the same then their practices should be the same, which they emphatically are not!! Even the crude indices of an EEG show tremendous differences, on which I will elaborate subsequently. Remember, I started to go to church for the anointing on the service as Brother Tucker accurately pegged. I read the Bible at this point in my venture with Christianity, but I only read the Gospels, because I considered Jesus to be a 'great teacher' and therefore worthy of my reading what he had to say. However, I refused to regard anything Paul wrote in the Bible because it was a well-known "fact" circulated among all those I had ever associated with that Paul was a misogynist!! That is, he hated women. What a lie! But I didn't know it then. In spite of the slow acceptance that I had of God and a relationship with Him, He kept leading me.

    I began to research professional psychology articles on the studies of psycho-physiological indices of religious practices. I found ample literature on Buddhist, yoga and Hindu practices, but almost none on Christian practices. I set my course for following two tracks of research for my study: one was literature research and the other was psycho-physiological in the form of studying electro-encephalographic correlates (EEG) of live subjects. This process of doing a study with live subjects was to entail an interesting combination of efforts. The university had an old chart recorder EEG, but, I never did like the detail work of analyzing miles of strip charts. I looked around and found some electro-encephalographic biofeedback equipment that was not being used and upon inspection found it had outputs for the amplitude and the frequency on two channels and it used DC voltage. The Psychology Department had a computer with 16k of memory, which they lovingly called "The Pet". Wow, what could a guy do with those machines? The Pet had input ports, one of which was a parallel port. So I went down to the EE department, and enlisted the aide of an engineer, Bob Rinker and a Technician. Between us, we designed an Analog to Digital Converter and then I built it. This converter put out a signal that the Pet could record. Programming the Pet was easy. The machine was capable of calculating and storing data sixteen times a second, which in today's computer world would be equivalent to a kiddie toy, but it was adequate for my purposes.

An interesting aspect of the study came when I was writing the software. My original premise was that speaking in tongues should produce the same brainwave results and feeling of well-being as Transcendental Meditation. Therefore, I was only going to look for, and store data for the same type of mental activity that had been observed in those studies: alpha wave and beta wave activity. But something in my gut prompted me to look a little deeper, so I put in another subroutine that looked for and stored theta wave activity.

One of the problems I encountered in conducting this study was getting spirit-filled subjects that would be agreeable to pray in tongues while I tested their brain wave activity. One of my good friends indicated that he thought that it was wrong to study the things of God, and declined to participate. I really feel that this brought the end of our friendship, and it still saddens my heart today, over twenty years later. However, I was able to get a total of six volunteers from two different churches in Moscow: the Assembly of God volunteers, and the closet charismatics from St Augustine's parish of the Roman Catholic Church. (I call them the Closet Charismatics because they weren't very large in number and used the cloakroom for their meetings.)

To put it in a nutshell, the experiment measured the electrical activity of both sides of the brain while the Christians were resting, then praying, then resting. The first period of five minutes they were asked to just sit quietly. The second period was fifteen minutes long and the Christians were asked to pray for that period of time as they would normally pray. If they prayed in tongues or if they prayed in their own language, they were to just pray as they normally would. Some prayed in English, then tongues, and back and forth as they wished, or were led by the Holy Spirit. One prayed in tongues the whole time. The software looked at three different types of brainwaves, alpha, beta, and theta. Below is a general definition of all three types of brainwaves, when they are predominantly found, and what they produce:

Alpha waves are commonly detected by electroencephalography (EEG) or magnetoencephalography (MEG) and predominantly found to originate from the occipital lobe during periods of relaxation, with eyes closed but still awake. Conversely alpha waves are attenuated with open eyes as well as by drowsiness and sleep. They are thought to represent the activity of the visual cortex in an idle state.

Beta wave, or beta rhythm, is the term used to designate the frequency range of brain activity above 12 Hz (12 transitions or cycles per second). Beta states are the states associated with normal waking consciousness. Low amplitude beta with multiple and varying frequencies is often associated with active, busy or anxious thinking and active concentration

Theta rhythms are normally absent in healthy awake adults but are physiological and natural in awake children under the age of 13 years. Theta waves are normally present just before sleep, what is referred to as the twilight state: between consciousness and sleep. It is associated with increased creativity, stress reduction, learning enhancement, and an awakening of intuition and other extrasensory perception skills.

My findings astounded me and dispelled my long-held belief that all religions are essentially the same. I expected to find similar results to what the proponents of TM touted as benefits of their form of meditation in that I expected to find increased alpha waves, however, what I found to my amazement was a marked increase in theta wave activity! The glossolalic activity (praying in tongues or a prayer language) was producing a state of mind that contributed to the subjects being receptive to more creativity, heightened learning capability, less stress, greater intuition and even ESP- related activities and moreover, the subject could choose to go there by entering into glossolalia!

At the time I interpreted my findings as happening because of the belief system of the subjects and wrote this in my thesis: "... increase in theta may be understood in relation to the glossolalists belief system. As already mentioned the glossolalists believe that the Holy Spirit is the author of this speech and that the spirit intercedes for and undertakes to rectify their problems. It is this belief that something is going to happen for the betterment of the individual, which allows the idea or solution to come to fruition in the individual's mind... Any insights and creative thought that might be associated with theta production would be a factor that would tend to reinforce glossolalic behavior. Such an increase of insight, particularly with respect to oneself, could be of value in attaining the goal of sinless perfection, as sought by Christian glossolalists, which is embodied in the example of Jesus Christ. An increase of creative thought would also be of value in the process of daily living. Therefore, no matter how this phenomenon is acquired, the insight and creativity would reinforce the behavior once it was acquired."

(If you would like to read my entire thesis, it is at the University of Idaho Library stored away some where. The title is, "Some Electroencephalographic Correlates of Glossolalic Christian Prayer.")

After decades of growing in my relationship with God, I now know that praying in tongues is a means by which The Lord provides edification and increased benefit for the life of the believer. I guess the Lord knew someone like me could accept it best from scientific data. Although my data sampling was small, it still produced a documented, verifiable result that substantiates the claims of the Bible. The entire years of time spent at the U of I have sharpened my perspectives on the role of science and how it relates to our daily lives. Although, I signed up in the field of Psychology and really didn't know why I was supposed to go into that discipline, God had a plan for my life that was way beyond anything I could imagine!

"But you, dear friends, build yourselves up in your most holy faith and pray in the Holy Spirit." Jude: 20

"Meanwhile, the moment we get tired in the waiting, God's Spirit is right alongside helping us along. If we don't know how or what to pray, it doesn't matter. He does our praying in and for us, making prayer out of our wordless sighs, our aching groans. He knows us far better than we know ourselves, knows our pregnant condition,

and keeps us present before God. That's why we can be so sure that every detail in our lives of love for God is worked into something good." Romans 8:26-28 (MSG)

CONCLUSION

    The events related in the previous sections are all true; however these stories are only a small sampling of the events in my life. When looking at the evil and the sin of the past there is a tendency to get caught up in the stories and feed on them rather than focusing on the Savior. With that in mind, I have kept my examples brief and sordid details to a minimum, but let me summarize all of my life without Christ by saying it was a life devoid of peace, both inner peace and outer as my life was full of chaos in the events surrounding me. It was not life, but rather existence.

    The greatest cry of my heart was, "I want to go home". Where was home? I could not answer that question for a very long time. As I accepted the Lord into my life and began to be delivered from some of the addictions that had held me captive even without my being aware of their existence, I began gradually to understand that my home is in Christ. He alone has set me at peace and given order and significance to the events of my world. He is indeed my hero because He has rescued me, delivered me, and given me the means to run my race of life—to win!

Is my story so sensational? Not really. Jesus is sensational. He meets us wherever we are; there is no pit too deep for His arms to reach down and pull us out.

There are several truths that I hope came out in Stories of a Salvation:

1) For those who are seeking the truth about God and not sure of His existence, be assured He is there. Sometimes our arrogance gets in the way of seeing Him. Ask him to reveal Himself to you and then take it as fact that He is on the case. He does not need us to find Him, He finds us.
2) For those who are full of hurt and pain imposed on you by those that should have loved you and protected you, Jesus knows your cries, even those that were not uttered—the ones deep inside your gut, too painful to share with any human being. He can and wants to heal that hurt of abandonment, the betrayal, the shock of human cruelty, the shame. He is not an imposter like the drugs that were touted in decades past, but He is the lover of our soul. He is the One who can heal the pain and turn our lives into something beautiful!
3) For those who have felt the sting of rejection from society as I have; those who have been labeled loosers, dead-beat dads, outcasts, hopeless cases, felons: know that you are prized by Jesus Christ.

CONCLUSION

You are of immeasurable value to Him, so much so that He paid the ultimate price for you. You are not stuck on that dead-end road. He has a plan for your life that includes acceptance, love, freedom from the past, and a purpose for the future. Grab a hold of it and don't let go!

4) For those who know He exists, but are still trying to get to a place where you can be acceptable to Him before you "become a Christian", forget it! None of us will ever be good enough in ourselves, but the gift of God is that He sent His son to pay the price for our soul even when we were unlovely and full of sin. So, stop trying and just accept the gift. Let Him be the God; he does a much better job at it than you and He has been doing it a long time already.

5) For those who are Christians, but find that you are still struggling with issues and your life seems to fluctuate like the tide, crashing and ebbing, crashing and ebbing, I say don't give up! Find a good Bible teaching church; read the Bible and let the truths sink into your life. We tend to think in our instant society that when we come to Christ our lives should suddenly be perfect and we are disappointed when they are not. Some things take time. Give God time. He doesn't bop us on the head and give up on us the first time we are presented with the idea of Him. So give Him ample time to undo all the mess you've made of your life. Your part is reading His words in the

Bible, His part is the rest.

Most importantly, God is faithful! He is faithful to be there for us and to meet us at our point of need. He is what He says He is, and does what He says He will do. Don't give up! If there was hope for this abusive, drinking, cussing, drugging, rowdy, don't-back-down-from-a-fight hippie, then, believe me, there is hope, brother, there is always hope!

CONCLUSION

WANT TO KNOW HOW TO ASK JESUS INTO YOUR LIFE?

1) Read through these verses from the Bible:

John 3:3 *"In reply Jesus declared, "I tell you the truth, no one can see the kingdom of God unless he is born again."*

John 3:16, 17 *"For God so loved the world that he gave his one and only Son, that whoever believes in him shall not perish but have eternal life. For God did not send his Son into the world to condemn the world, but to save the world through him."*

Romans 3:23 *"for all have sinned and fall short of the glory of God"*
This is the reason we must be born again.

Romans 6:23 *"For the wages of sin is death, but the gift of God is eternal life in Christ Jesus our Lord."*
Eternal life is a gift from God. You cannot earn it on your own.

Romans 10:9 *"That if you confess with your mouth, "Jesus is Lord, and believe in your heart that God raised him from the dead, you will be saved."*
Being saved or born again is receiving Jesus as your Lord

(Master), and committing yourself to follow His Word (the Bible).

2) Say this prayer:

> "God, I come to You in the Name of Jesus. I ask You to come into my life. I confess with my mouth that Jesus is Lord and I believe in my heart that You have raised Him from the dead. I turn my back on sin and I commit to follow You for the rest of my life. I thank You, Father, for saving me!"

You are now born again, forgiven, and on your way to heaven. You are a new creation! Yet this is only the beginning. It is important to renew your mind to live a powerful life as a believer. Obtain a Bible and read the following verses to start you on your new path.

II Corinthians 5:17 You are a new creation

Romans 12:2 Renew your mind to live a powerful life as a believer.

Romans 10:17 Reading the Bible is important to your growth.

Hebrews 10:25 Getting together with believers regularly is vital

Conclusion

Acts 10:48 It's important to be baptized in water as a believer

John 14:26 Being filled with the Holy Spirit is another gift God wants to give to you. You need His power in order to live the Christian life God wants you to live.

*If you ever have doubts about your salvation, reject them, and remember that regardless of your emotions or how you feel, you are saved because you obeyed Romans 10:9.

POST CONCLUSION

Even though there is a conclusion in this book, it should really be called the intermission. One thing that strikes me in recent times is that on occasion when I have told some of these events, I am asked, "When was this?" I tell them most of these particular events happened in the seventies. Then their response is something like, "Oh. I thought so.", as if that was the time when God was awake. It is as if they are almost implying that since then God has gone to sleep, or on vacation, or some such thing has happened and they don't expect to hear of stories like these since the seventies. However, we know that we serve an unchanging God.

"Jesus Christ the same yesterday, and to day, and for ever."
Heb 13:8 (KJV)

Since this is true, we should see more amazing things of God, and indeed I have. *Stories of a Salvation* encompasses only the beginning of the journey in an on-going, life-long relationship with Jesus Christ where we continually see the reality of Jesus Christ working in and through our lives. Through the power of Jesus Christ and through the working of the Holy Spirit, I was able to overcome some big things in my life, but these were only the tip of the iceberg in my case. Anger, rage, and abusive behavior have been the most difficult things to overcome in my life and they have taken much longer to be free from. But Praise be to the Lord because He is bigger than any sin, any behavior, any place in life that we feel we are stuck!

Statistics say in most cases overcoming anger and abuse are less often overcome than drugs and alcohol. I have had a professional counselor tell me that those people that have undergone as much traumatic abuse as I have usually have gone to prison for much of their lives. But with God, it is possible to be set free from abuse and no longer be an abuser. Don't miss the next installment of Stories of a Salvation.